Learning the vi Editor

Books That Help People Get More Out of Computers

Learning the vi Editor, 5th Edition, 192 pages
By Linda Lamb

Complete guide to text editing with *vi*, the editor available on nearly every UNIX system. Early chapters cover the basics; later chapters explain more advanced editing tools, such as *ex* commands and global search and replacement.

Typesetting Tables on the UNIX System, 280 pages
By Henry McGilton and Mary McNabb

For those UNIX users who depend on *troff*, the definitive guide to *tbl*. If you're a novice UNIX user, this book is the best way to learn *tbl*. If you're an expert, the book will pay for itself the first time you want to show off.

sed & awk, 414 pages
By Dale Dougherty

For people who create and modify text files, *sed* and *awk* are power tools for editing. Most of the things that you can do with these programs can be done interactively with a text editor. However, using *sed* and *awk* can save many hours of repetitive work in achieving the same result.

UNIX Text Processing, 665 pages
By Dale Dougherty & Tim O'Reilly

Published by MacMillan Books, but written by yours truly, this comprehensive book tells you all you'll ever need to know about UNIX text processing, from basic editing to writing complex *troff* macro packages.

Learning the vi Editor

Linda Lamb

O'Reilly & Associates, Inc.
632 Petaluma Avenue
Sebastopol, CA 95472

Learning the vi Editor
by Linda Lamb

Nutshell Series Editor Tim O'Reilly

Copyright © 1990 O'Reilly & Associates, Inc.
All rights reserved.

Printed in the United States of America.

Printing History

Feb. 1986:   1st edition, by Linda Lamb.

April 1986:   2nd edition, with minor corrections.

Aug. 1987:   3rd edition; revised and enlarged, index added, by Walter
                Gallant. Revised page design by Linda Lamb and Dale
                Dougherty.

June 1988:   4th edition; updated, minor corrections by Tim O'Reilly.

Oct. 1990:   5th edition; revised and enlarged by Daniel Gilly.

Please address comments and questions in care of the publisher:

O'Reilly & Associates, Inc.
632 Petaluma Avenue
Sebastopol, CA 95472
in USA 1-800-338-6887
international +1 707-829-0515

UUCP: uunet!ora!nuts
Internet: nuts@ora.com

Table of Contents

Page

Preface to the 5th Edition xi

Preface xiii

Scope of This Handbook xiii
The Nutshell Format xiv
  Discussion of vi Commands xiv
  Typefaces xiv
  Keystrokes xv
  Problem Checklist xvi
What You Need to Know Before Starting xvi

Chapter 1 The vi Text Editor 1

Opening and Closing Files 3
  Opening a File 4
  Problems Opening Files 5
  Saving and Quitting a File 6
Quitting Without Saving Edits 7
  Problems Saving Files 8

Chapter 2 Simple Editing 10

vi Commands 11
Moving the Cursor 12
  Single Movements 13
  Numeric Arguments 14
  Movement Within a Line 14
  Movement by Text Blocks 15
Simple Edits 16
  Inserting New Text 18
  Appending Text 19
  Changing Text 20

Changing Case 23
Deleting Text 23
Moving Text 27
Copying Text 29
Repeating or Undoing Your Last Command 31
More Ways to Insert Text 33
Numeric Arguments for Insert Commands 34
Joining Two Lines with J 34
Problem Checklist 35
Review of Basic vi Commands 35

Chapter 3 Moving Around in a Hurry 37

Movement by Screens 38
Scrolling the Screen 38
Scrolling with z 39
Redrawing the Screen 39
Movement Within a Screen 40
Movement by Line 41
Movement by Text Blocks 41
Movement by Searches 42
Repeating Searches 44
Current Line Searches 45
Movement by Line Number 46
The G (Go To) Command 47

Chapter 4 Beyond the Basics 49

More Command Combinations 50
Options When Starting vi 51
Advancing to a Specific Place 51
Read-only Mode 52
Recovering a Buffer 53
Making Use of Buffers 54
Recovering Deletions 55
Yanking to Named Buffers 55
Marking Your Place 57
Other Advanced Edits 57

Chapter 5 Introducing the ex Editor 58

ex Commands 59
   Problem Checklist 61
Editing with ex 62
   Line Addresses 62
   Defining a Range of Lines 63
   Line Addressing Symbols 64
   Search Patterns 65
   Redefining the Current Line Position 66
   Global Searches 67
   Combining ex Commands 68
Saving and Exiting Files 68
   Renaming the Buffer 69
   Saving Part of a File 69
   Appending to a Saved File 70
Copying a File into Another File 70
Editing Multiple Files 71
   Invoking vi on Multiple Files 71
   Calling In New Files 72
   Edits Between Files 74

Chapter 6 Global Replacement 76

Confirming Substitutions 78
Context-sensitive Replacement 79
Pattern-matching Rules 80
   Metacharacters Used in Search Patterns 81
   Metacharacters Used in Replacement Strings 83
Pattern-matching Examples 85
   Search for General Class of Words 87
   Block Move by Patterns 87
   More Examples 89
   A Final Look at Pattern Matching 95

Chapter 7 Advanced Editing 102

Customizing vi 103
    The :set Command 104
    The .exrc File 105
    Alternate Environments 106
    Some Useful Options 107
Executing UNIX Commands 108
    Filtering Text Through a Command 109
Saving Commands 112
    Word Abbreviation 112
    Using the map Command 114
    Protecting Keys from Interpretation by ex 115
    Complex Mapping Example 116
    More Examples of Mapping Keys 117
    Mapping Keys for Insert Mode 120
    Mapping Function Keys 121
    Mapping Other Special Keys 123
    @-Functions 123
Using ex Scripts 124
    Looping in a Shell Script 126
    Here Documents 128
    Sorting Text Blocks: A Sample ex Script 129
    Comments in ex Scripts 130
    ex Scripts Built by diff 131
    Where to Go from Here 134
Editing Program Source Code 134
    Indentation Control 135
    A Special Search Command 136
    Using Tags 137

Appendix A Quick Reference 139

Movement Commands 140
Editing Commands 142
Exit Commands 143
Command Line Options 144
Other ex Commands 144

Appendix B Setting Environment Options 146

Appendix C ex commands 151

Command Syntax 151
    Address Symbols 152
    Option Symbols 152
Alphabetical List of Commands 153

Appendix D Problem Checklist 161

Problems Opening Files 161
Problems Saving Files 163
Problems Getting to Visual Mode 164
Problems with vi Commands 165
Problems with Deletions 165

Index 166

Preface
to the 5th Edition

The 5th edition of *Learning the vi Editor* contains many improvements. We have expanded the treatment of existing topics, and we have added some completely new topics and features:

1. *The book has a quick-reference guide to all commands.*

   This guide, located at the back of the book, can be pulled out and used as a handy reference card.

2. *ex editor commands are discussed more fully.*

   In Chapters 5, 6, and 7, the complex features of *ex* and *vi* have been clarified by adding more examples, in topics such as regular expression syntax, global replacement, *.exrc* files, word abbreviations, keyboard maps, and editing scripts.

A few of the examples are drawn from articles in *UNIX World* magazine. Walter Zintz wrote a two-part tutorial* on *vi* that taught us a few things we didn't know, and that also had a lot of clever examples illustrating features we did already cover in the book. Ray Swartz had a helpful tip in one of his columns.† We are grateful for the ideas in these articles.

The increased emphasis on *ex* warranted a summary of all *ex* commands, so we added an alphabetical listing in Appendix C, *ex commands*.

3. *Minor additions or corrections* have been made to the discussions of basic *vi* commands. Many of these additions are based on comments by Kismet McDonough of O'Reilly & Associates, Inc., and by Steve Simmons, who teaches *vi* on the West Coast. The comments were very useful.

The following people at O'Reilly & Associates, Inc. worked on the 5th edition: Daniel Gilly wrote most of the new material; Mike Sierra produced the manuscript; and Chris Reilley designed the quick-reference guide and redesigned the original figures.

---

* "*vi* Tips for Power Users," *UNIX World*, April 1990; and "Using *vi* to Automate Complex Edits," *UNIX World*, May 1990. Both articles by Walter Zintz.

† "Answers to UNIX," *UNIX World*, August 1990.

Preface

Scope of This Handbook
The Nutshell Format
What You Need to Know Before Starting

Text editing is one of the most common uses of any computer system, and *vi* is one of the most useful standard text editors on your system. With *vi* you can create new files, or edit any existing UNIX text file.

Scope of This Handbook

This book is designed to get you started using *vi* quickly, and to follow up with advanced skills that will let you use it effectively. The first two chapters, *The vi Text Editor* and *Simple Editing*, present some simple *vi* commands with which you can get started. You should practice these until they are second nature. You could stop at the end of Chapter 2, having learned some elementary editing tools.

But *vi* is meant to do a lot more than rudimentary word processing; the variety of commands and options enables you to shortcut a lot of editing drudgery. Chapters 3 and 4 concentrate on easier ways to do tasks. For a first reading, get at least an idea of what *vi* can do and what commands you might harness for your specific uses. Later, you can come back to these chapters for further study.

Chapters 5, 6, and 7 provide tools that help you shift more of the editing burden to the computer. They introduce you to the *ex* line editor underlying *vi*, and show you how to issue *ex* commands from within *vi*.

The appendices provide useful reference material on *vi* commands, *ex* commands, and options available to *vi*.

The Nutshell Format

The philosophy of this handbook is to give you a good overview of what we feel are *vi* survival materials for the new user. Learning a new editor, especially an editor with all the options of *vi*, can seem like an overwhelming task. We have made an effort to present basic concepts and commands in an easy-to-read and logical manner. The following sections describe the conventions used in this handbook.

Discussion of vi Commands

A picture of a keyboard button, like the one on the left, marks the main discussion of that particular keyboard command or of related commands. You will find a brief introduction to the main concept before it is broken down into task-oriented sections. The appropriate command to use in each case is then presented, along with a description of the command and the proper syntax for using it.

Typefaces

In syntax descriptions and examples, what you would actually type is shown in the `Courier` font, as are all command names. Variables (which you would not type literally, but would replace with an actual value when you typed the command) are shown in *Courier italics*. Brackets indicate that a variable is optional. For example, in the syntax line:

    vi [*filename*]

filename would be replaced by an actual filename. The brackets indicate that the `vi` command can be invoked without specifying a filename at all. The brackets themselves are not typed.

Certain examples show the effect of commands typed at the UNIX shell prompt. In such examples, what you actually type is shown in **Courier Bold** to distinguish it from the system response. For example:

    $ **ls**
    ch01 ch02 ch03 ch04

In examples, *italics* are used to indicate a comment which is not to be typed. Otherwise, *italics* are used for emphasizing special terms and for the names of files.

Keystrokes

Special keystrokes are shown in a box. For example:

    i**With** a ⌷ESC⌷

Throughout this handbook, you will also find columns of *vi* commands and their results:

Keystrokes   **Result**

Z Z

┌──┐
│ "practice" [New file] 6 lines, 320 characters   │
└──┘

Give the write and save command, Z Z. Your file is saved as a regular UNIX file.

In the example above, the command Z Z is shown in the left column. In the window to the right is a line (or several lines) of the screen that show the result of the command. Cursor position is shown by an underscore. In this instance, since Z Z saves and writes the file, you see the status line shown when a file is written; cursor position is not shown. Below the window is an explanation of the command and its result.

Sometimes *vi* commands are issued by pressing the CTRL key and another key simultaneously. In the text, this combination keystroke is written within a box (for example, CTRL-G). In examples, it is written by preceding the name of the key with a caret (^). For example, ^G means to hold down CTRL while pressing the *g* key.

Problem Checklist

√   A problem checklist is included in those sections where you may run into some trouble. You can skim these checklists and go back to them when you actually encounter a problem. All of the problem checklists are also collected in Appendix D for ease of reference.

What You Need to Know Before Starting

This booklet assumes you have already read the Nutshell Handbook, *Learning the UNIX Operating System*, or some other introduction to UNIX. You should already know how to:

* Log in and log out.
* Enter UNIX commands.
* Change directories.
* List files in a directory.
* Create, copy, and remove files.

Familiarity with grep (a global search program) and wildcard characters is also helpful.

Although *vi* can run on almost any terminal, it must know what kind of terminal you are using. The terminal type is usually set in your *.profile* or *.login* file. See your system administrator if you are not sure whether your terminal type is defined correctly. This will avoid possible confusion for you when you start experimenting with *vi*.

The vi Text Editor
Opening and Closing Files
Quitting Without Saving Edits

UNIX has a number of editors that can process the contents of text files, whether those files contain data, source code, or sentences. There are line editors, such as *ed* and *ex*, which display a line of the file on the screen; and there are screen editors, such as *vi* and *emacs*, which display a part of the file on your terminal screen.

vi is the most useful standard text editor on your system. (*vi* is short for *vi*sual editor and is pronounced "vee-eye.") Unlike *emacs*, it is available in nearly identical form on nearly every UNIX system, thus providing a kind of text-editing *lingua franca*. The same might be said of *ed* and *ex*, but screen editors are generally much easier to use. With a screen editor you can scroll the page, move the cursor, delete lines, insert characters, and more, while seeing the results of your edits as you make them. Screen editors are very popular, since they allow you to make changes as you read through a file, much as you would edit a printed copy, only faster.

To many beginners, *vi* looks unintuitive and cumbersome—instead of using special control keys for word processing functions and just letting you type normally, it uses all of the regular keyboard keys for issuing commands. When the keyboard keys are issuing commands, *vi* is said to be in *command mode*. You must be in a special *insert mode* before you can type actual text on the screen. In addition, there seem to be so many commands.

Once you start learning, however, you realize that *vi* is well-designed. You need only a few keystrokes to tell *vi* to do complex tasks. As you learn *vi*, you learn shortcuts that transfer more and more of the editing work to the computer—where it belongs.

vi (like any text editor) is not a "what you see is what you get" word processor. If you want to produce formatted documents, you must type in codes that are used by another formatting program to control the appearance of the printed copy. If you want to indent several paragraphs, for instance, you put a code where the indent begins and ends. Formatting codes allow you to experiment with or change the appearance of your printed files, and in many ways, give you much more control over the appearance of your documents than a word processor. UNIX supports the *nroff/troff* formatting package.

(*vi* does support some simple formatting mechanisms. For example, you can tell it to automatically wrap when you come to the end of a line, or to automatically indent new lines.)

As with any skill, the more editing you do, the easier the basics become, and the more you can accomplish. Once you are used to all the powers you have while editing with *vi*, you may never want to return to any "simpler" editor.

What are the components of editing? First, you want to *insert* text (a forgotten word or a missing sentence), and you want to *delete* text (a stray character or an entire paragraph). You also need to *change* letters and words (to correct misspellings or to reflect a change of mind about a term). You might want to *move* text from one place to another part of your file. And, on occasion, you want to *copy* text to duplicate it in another part of your file.

Unlike many word processors, *vi*'s command mode is the initial or "default" mode. Complex, interactive edits can be performed with only a few keystrokes. (And to insert raw text, you simply give any of the several "insert" commands and then type away.)

One or two characters are used for the basic commands. For example:

i   insert
cw   change word

Using letters as commands, you can edit a file with great speed. You don't have to memorize banks of function keys or stretch your fingers to reach awkward combinations of keys. Most of the commands can be remembered by the letter that performs them, and nearly all commands follow similar patterns and are related to each other.

In general, *vi* commands:

- Are case-sensitive (uppercase and lowercase keystrokes mean different things; I is different from i).
- Are not shown (or "echoed") on the screen when you type them.
- Do not require a RETURN after the command.

There is also a group of commands that echo on the bottom line of the screen. Bottom-line commands are preceded by different symbols. The slash (/) and the question mark (?) begin search commands, which are discussed in Chapter 3, *Moving Around in a Hurry*. A colon (:) begins all *ex* commands. *ex* commands are those that are used by the *ex* line editor. The *ex* editor is available to you when you use *vi*, because *ex* is the underlying editor, and *vi* is really just its "visual" mode. *ex* commands and concepts are discussed fully in Chapter 5, *Introducing the ex Editor*, but this chapter introduces you to the *ex* commands to quit a file without saving edits.

Opening and Closing Files

You can use *vi* to edit any text file. *vi* copies the file to be edited into a *buffer* (an area temporarily set aside in memory), displays the buffer (though you can see only one screenful at a time), and lets you add, delete and change text. When you save your edits, *vi* copies the edited buffer back into a permanent file, replacing the old file of the same name. Remember that you are always working on a *copy* of your file in the buffer, and that your edits will not affect your original file until you save the buffer. Saving your edits is also called "writing the buffer," or more commonly "writing your file."

Opening a File

 vi is the UNIX command that invokes the *vi* editor for an existing file or for a brand new file. The syntax for the vi command is:

$ **vi** [*filename*]

The brackets shown on the above command line indicate that the filename is optional. The brackets should not be typed. The $ is the UNIX prompt. If the filename is omitted, *vi* will open an unnamed buffer. You can assign the name when you write the buffer into a file. For right now, though, let's stick to naming the file on the command line.

A filename must be unique inside its directory. On a System V UNIX system, it cannot exceed 14 characters in length (Berkeley UNIX systems allow up to 64 characters). A filename can include any ASCII character except a slash (/), which is reserved as the separator between files and directories in a pathname. You can even include spaces in a filename by typing a backslash (\) before the space. In practice, though, filenames generally consist of any combination of uppercase and lowercase letters, numbers, and the characters dot (.) and underscore (_). Remember that UNIX is case-sensitive: lowercase letters are distinct from uppercase letters. Also remember that you must press [RETURN] to signal to UNIX that you are finished issuing your command.

When you want to open a new file in a directory, give a new filename with the vi command. For example, if you wanted to open a new file called *practice* in the current directory, you would enter:

$ **vi practice**

Since this is a new file, the buffer is empty and the screen appears as follows:

```
~
~
~
"practice" [New file].
```

The tildes (~) down the left-hand column of the screen indicate that there is no text in the file, not even blank lines. The prompt line (also called the status line) at the bottom of the screen echoes the name and status of the file.

You can also edit any existing text file in a directory by specifying its filename. Suppose that there is a UNIX file with the pathname */usr/john/letter*. If you are already in the */usr/john* directory, use the relative pathname. For example:

```
$ vi letter
```

brings a copy of the file *letter* to the screen.

If you are in another directory, give the full pathname to begin editing:

```
$ vi /usr/john/letter
```

Problems Opening Files

√ *When you invoke* vi, *the message* [open mode] *appears.*

Your terminal type is probably incorrectly identified. Quit the editing session immediately by typing :q and ask your system administrator to provide an adequate terminal type setting.

√ *You see one of the following messages:*

```
Visual needs addressable cursor or upline capability
Bad termcap entry
Termcap entry too long
terminal:  Unknown terminal type
Block device required
Not a typewriter
```

Your terminal type is either undefined, or there's probably something wrong with your *termcap* or *terminfo* entry. Enter :q to quit. Then ask your system administrator to select a terminal type for your environment.

√ *A* [new file] *message appears when you think a file already exists.*

You are probably in the wrong directory. Enter :q to quit. Then check to see that you are in the correct directory for that file (enter pwd at the UNIX prompt). If you are in the right directory, check the list of files in the directory (with ls) to see whether the file exists under a slightly different name.

√ *You invoke* vi, *but you get a colon prompt (indicating that you're in* ex *line-editing mode).*

You probably typed an interrupt before *vi* could draw the screen. Enter *vi* by typing `vi` at the *ex* prompt (`:`).

√ *One of the following messages appears:*

```
[Read only]
File is read only
Permission denied
```

"Read only" means that you can only look at the file; you cannot save any changes you make. You may have invoked *vi* in *view mode* (with `view` or `vi -R`), or you do not have write permission for the file. See the section "Problems Saving Files" below.

√ *One of the following messages appears:*

```
Bad file number
Block special file
Character special file
Directory
Executable
Non-ascii file
file non-ASCII
```

The file you've called up to edit is not a regular text file.

√ *When you type* `:q` *because of one of the above difficulties, the message appears:*

```
No write since last change (:quit! overrides).
```

You have modified the file without realizing it. Type `:q!` to leave *vi*. Your changes from this session will not be saved in the file.

Saving and Quitting a File

You can quit working on a file at any time, save your edits and return to the UNIX prompt. The *vi* command to quit and save edits is `ZZ`. Note that `ZZ` is capitalized.

Let's assume that you do create a file called *practice* to practice *vi* commands, and that you type in six lines of text. To save the file, first check that you are in command mode by pressing ESC, and then enter ZZ.

Keystrokes   **Result**

ZZ

```
"practice" [New file] 6 lines, 320 characters
```

Give the write and save command, ZZ. Your file is saved as a regular UNIX file.

ls

```
ch01          ch02          practice
```

Listing the files in the directory shows the new file *practice* that you created.

You can also save your edits with *ex* commands. Type :w to save your file but not quit *vi*; type :q to quit if you haven't made any edits; and type :wq to both quit and save your edits. (:wq is equivalent to ZZ.) We'll explain fully how to use commands in Chapter 5, *Introducing the ex Editor*; for now, you should just memorize a few commands for writing and saving files.

Quitting Without Saving Edits

When you are first learning *vi*, especially if you are an intrepid experimenter, there are two other *ex* commands that are handy for getting out of any mess that you might create.

What if you want to wipe out all of the edits you have made in a session and then return to the original file? The command:

    :e! RETURN

reads the original copy of the file back in, so you can start over.

Suppose, however, that you want to wipe out your edits and then just quit *vi*? The command:

> :q! [RETURN]

quits the file you're editing and returns you to the UNIX prompt. With both of these commands, you lose all edits made in the buffer since the last time you saved the file. *vi* normally won't let you throw away your edits. The exclamation point added to the :e or :q command causes *vi* to override this prohibition, performing the operation even though the buffer has been modified.

Problems Saving Files

√ *You try to write your file, but you get one of the following messages:*

```
File exists
File file exists - use w!
[Existing file]
File is read only
```

Type :w! *file* to overwrite the existing file, or type :w! *newfile* to save the edited version in a new file.

√ *You want to write a file, but you don't have write permission for it. You get the message "Permission denied."*

Use :w! *newfile* to write out the buffer into a new file. If you have write permission for the directory, you can use mv to replace the original version with your copy of it. If you don't have write permission for the directory, type :w! *pathname/file* to write out the buffer to a directory in which you do have write permission (such as your home directory).

√ *You try to write your file, but you get a message telling you that the file system is full.*

Type :!df to see whether there's any space on another file system. If there is, choose a directory on that file system and write your file to it with :w! *pathname*. (Starting an *ex* command with an exclamation point gives you access to UNIX, and df is the UNIX command to check a disk's free space.)

√ *The system puts you into open mode and tells you that the file system is full.*

The disk with *vi*'s temporary files is filled up. Type : ! ls /tmp to see whether there are any files you can remove to gain some disk space. If there are, create a temporary UNIX shell from which you can remove files or issue other UNIX commands. You can create a shell by typing : sh; type CTRL-D or exit to terminate the shell and return to *vi*. (On a Berkeley UNIX system, you can simply type CTRL-Z to suspend *vi* and return to the UNIX prompt; type % to return to *vi*.) Once you've freed up some space, write your file with : w !.

√ *You try to write your file, but you get a message telling you that your disk quota has been reached.*

Try to force the system to save your buffer with the *ex* command : pre (short for : preserve). If that doesn't work, look for some files to remove. Use : sh (or CTRL-Z if you are using a Berkeley system) to move out of *vi* and remove files. Use CTRL-D (or %) to return to *vi* when you're done. Then write your file with : w !.

Exercise:

The only way to learn *vi* is to practice. You now know enough to create a new file and to return to the UNIX prompt. Create a file called *practice*, insert some text, and then save and quit the file.

Open a file called practice in the current directory	vi practice
Insert text	i any text you like
Return to command mode	ESC
Quit vi, saving edits	ZZ

2

Simple Editing

vi Commands
Moving the Cursor
Simple Edits
More Ways to Insert Text
Joining Two Lines with J
Review of Basic vi Commands

This chapter introduces you to editing with *vi*, and it is set up to be read as a tutorial. In it you will learn how to move the cursor and how to make some simple edits. If you've never worked with *vi*, you should read the entire chapter.

Later chapters show you how to expand your skills to perform faster and more powerful edits. One of the biggest advantages for an adept user of *vi* is that there are so many options to choose from. (One of the biggest *disadvantages* for a newcomer to *vi* is that there are so many different editor commands.)

You can't learn *vi* by memorizing every single *vi* command. Start out by learning the basic commands introduced in this chapter. Note the patterns of use that the commands have in common. As you learn *vi*, be on the lookout for more tasks that you can delegate to the editor, and then find the command that accomplishes it. In later chapters you will learn more advanced features of *vi*, but before you can handle the advanced, you must master the simple.

This chapter covers:

☐ Moving the cursor.

☐ Adding and changing text.

☐ Deleting, moving, and copying text.

☐ More ways to enter insert mode.

vi Commands

vi has two modes: command mode and insert mode. As soon as you enter a file, you are in command mode, and the editor is waiting for you to enter a command. Commands enable you to move anywhere in the file, to perform edits, or to enter insert mode to add new text. Commands can also be given to exit the file (saving or ignoring your edits) in order to return to the UNIX prompt.

You can think of the different modes as representing two different keyboards. In insert mode, your keyboard functions like a typewriter. In command mode, each key has a new meaning or initiates some instruction.

There are several ways to tell *vi* that you want to begin insert mode. One of the most common is to press i. The i doesn't appear on the screen, but after you press it, whatever you type *will* appear on the screen and will be entered into the buffer. The cursor marks the current insertion point. To tell *vi* that you want to stop inserting text, press ESC. Pressing ESC moves the cursor back one space (so that it is on the last character you typed) and returns *vi* to command mode.

For example, suppose you have opened a new file and want to insert the word "introduction". If you type the keystrokes iintroduction, what appears on the screen is:

```
introduction
```

When you open a new file, *vi* starts in command mode and interprets the first keystroke (i) as the insert command. All keystrokes made after the insert command are considered text until you press ESC. If you need to correct a mistake while in insert mode, backspace and type over the error. Depending on the type of terminal you are using, backspacing may erase what you've previously typed or may just back up over it. In either case, whatever you back up over will be deleted. Note that you can't use the backspace key to back up beyond the point where you entered insert mode.

vi has an option that lets you define a right margin and provides a carriage return automatically when you reach it. For right now, while you are inserting text, press RETURN to break the lines.

Sometimes you don't know whether you are in insert mode or command mode. Whenever *vi* does not respond as you expect, press ESC once or twice to check which mode you are in. When you hear the beep, you are in command mode.

Moving the Cursor

You may spend only a small amount of time in an editing session adding new text in insert mode; much of the time you will be making edits to existing text.

In command mode you can position the cursor anywhere in the file. Since you begin all basic edits (changing, deleting, and copying text) by placing the cursor at the text that you want to change, you want to be able to move the cursor to that place as quickly as possible.

There are *vi* commands to move the cursor:

• Up, down, left, or right—one *character* at a time.

• Forward or backward by blocks of *text* such as words, sentences, or paragraphs.

• Forward or backward through a file, one *screen* at a time.

In Figure 2-1, an underscore marks the present cursor position. Circles show movement of the cursor from its current position to the position that would result from various *vi* commands.

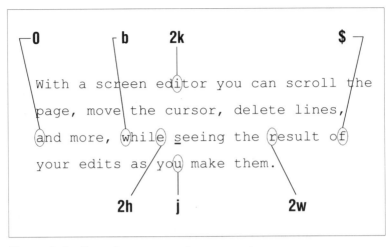

Figure 2-1. Sample movement commands

Single Movements

The keys h, j, k, and l, right under your fingertips, will move the cursor:

h	left, one space.
j	down, one line.
k	up, one line.
l	right, one space.

You can also use the cursor arrow keys (⬅️ ⬇️ ⬆️ ➡️) or the RETURN and BACKSPACE keys, but they are out of the way, and the arrow keys are not supported by all terminals. At first, it may seem awkward to use letter keys instead of arrows for cursor movement. After a short while, though, you'll find it is one of the things you'll like best about *vi*—you can move around without ever taking your fingers off the center of the keyboard.

Before you move the cursor, press ESC to make sure that you are in command mode. Use h, j, k, and l to move forward or backward in the file from the current cursor position. When you have gone as far as possible in one direction, you hear a beep and the cursor stops. For example, once you're at the beginning or end of a line, you cannot use h or l to wrap around to the previous or next line; you have to use j or k. Similarly, you cannot move the cursor past a tilde (˜)

representing a line without text, nor can you move the cursor above the first line of text.

Numeric Arguments

You can precede movement commands with numbers. Figure 2-2 shows how the command 4l moves the cursor four spaces to the right, just as if you had typed l four times (llll).

Figure 2-2. Multiplying commands by numbers

The ability to multiply commands gives you more options and power for each command you learn. Keep it in mind as you are introduced to additional commands.

Movement Within a Line

When you saved the file *practice*, *vi* displayed a message telling you how many lines are in that file. A *line* is not necessarily the same length as the visible line (limited usually to 80 characters) that appears on the screen. A line is any text entered between newlines. (A *new-line* character is inserted into the file when you press the RETURN key in insert mode.) If you type 200 characters before pressing RETURN, *vi* regards all 200 characters as a single line (even though those 200 characters visibly take up several lines on the screen).

As we mentioned, *vi* has an option that allows you to set a distance from the right margin at which *vi* will automatically insert a newline character. This option is wrapmargin (its abbreviation is wm). You can set a wrapmargin at 10 characters by typing:

        :set wm=10

This command doesn't affect lines that you've already typed. We'll talk more about setting options in Chapter 7, *Advanced Editing*. (This one really couldn't wait!)

If you do not use *vi*'s automatic `wrapmargin` option, you should break lines with carriage returns to keep the lines of manageable length.

Two useful commands that involve movement within a line are:

0   Move to beginning of line.

$ Move to end of line.

In the example below, line numbers are displayed. (Line numbers can be displayed in *vi* by using the `number` option, which is enabled by typing `:set nu` in command mode. This operation is described in Chapter 7, *Advanced Editing*.)

```
1   With a screen editor you can scroll the page,
2   move the cursor, delete lines, insert characters,
    and more, while seeing the results of your edits
    as you make them.
3   Screen editors are very popular.
```

The number of logical lines (3) does not correspond to the number of visible lines (5) that you see on the screen. If the cursor was positioned on the *d* in the word *delete*, and you entered $, the cursor would move to the period following the word *them*. If you entered 0, the cursor would move back to the letter *m* in the word *move*, at the beginning of line two.

Movement by Text Blocks

You can also move the cursor by blocks of text: words, sentences, paragraphs, etc.

The **w** command moves the cursor forward one word at a time, counting symbols and punctuation as equivalent to words. The line below shows cursor movement by **w**:

```
cursor, delete lines, insert characters,
```

You can also move by word, not counting symbols and punctuation, using the W command. (You can think of this as a "large" or "capital" *W*ord.) Cursor movement using W looks like this:

```
cursor, delete lines, insert characters,
```

To move backward by word, use the b command. Capital B allows you to move backward by word, not counting punctuation.

As mentioned previously, movement commands take numeric arguments; so, with either the w or b commands you can multiply the movement with numbers. 2w moves forward two words; 5B moves back five words, not counting punctuation.

We'll discuss movement by sentences and by paragraphs in Chapter 3, *Moving Around in a Hurry*. For now, practice using the cursor movement commands that you know, combining them with numeric multipliers.

Simple Edits

When you enter text in your file, it is rarely perfect. You find typos or want to improve on a phrase; sometimes your program has a bug. Once you enter text, you have to be able to change it, delete it, move it, or copy it. Figure 2-3 shows the kinds of edits you might want to make to a file. The edits are indicated by proofreading marks.

In *vi* you can perform any of these edits with a few basic keystrokes: i for insert (which you've already seen); a for append; c for change; and d for delete. To move or copy text, you use a pair of commands. You move text with a d for delete, then a p for put; you copy text with a y for "yank," then a p for put. Each type of edit is described in this section. Figure 2-4 shows the *vi* commands you use to make the edits marked in Figure 2-3.

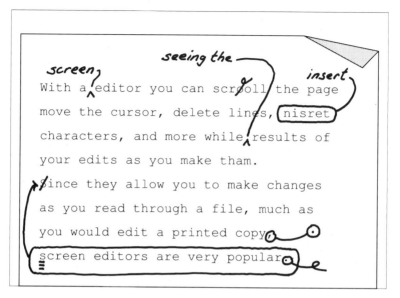

Figure 2-3. Proofreading edits

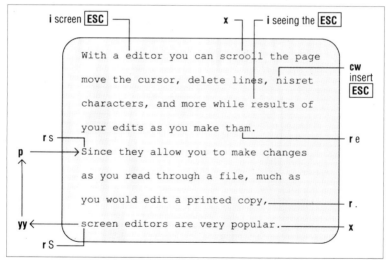

Figure 2-4. Edits with vi commands

Inserting New Text

You have already seen the insert command used to enter text into a new file. You also use the insert command while editing existing text to add missing characters, words, and sentences. In the file *practice*, suppose you have the sentence:

```
you can scroll
the page, move the cursor, delete
lines, and insert characters.
```

with the cursor positioned as shown. To insert *With a screen editor* at the beginning of the sentence, enter the following:

Keystrokes	**Result**

2 k

```
you can scroll
the page, move the cursor, delete
lines, and insert characters.
```

Move the cursor up two lines with the k command, to the line where you want to make the insertion.

i With a

```
With a you can scroll
the page, move the cursor, delete
lines, and insert characters.
```

Press i to enter insert mode and begin inserting text.

screen editor [ESC]

```
With a screen editor you can scroll
the page, move the cursor, delete
lines, and insert characters.
```

Finish inserting text, and press ESC to end the insert and return to command mode.

On the screen shown in the example above, *vi* pushes existing text to the right as the new text is inserted. That is because we are assuming that you are using *vi* on an "intelligent" terminal that can rewrite the screen with each character you type. An insert on a "dumb" terminal (such as an *adm3a*) will look different. The terminal itself cannot handle the overhead of updating the screen for each character typed (without a tremendous sacrifice of speed), so the terminal doesn't allow the screen to be rewritten until after you press ESC. On a dumb terminal, the same insert would appear:

Keystrokes   **Result**

iWith a
```
With an scroll
the page, move the cursor, delete
lines, and insert characters.
```

Press i to enter insert mode and begin inserting text. The dumb terminal appears to overwrite the existing text on the line.

screen editor
```
With a screen editor_
the page, move the cursor, delete
lines, and insert characters.
```

The insertion appears to have overwritten existing text.

ESC
```
With a screen editor_you can scroll
the page, move the cursor, delete
lines, and insert characters.
```

After you have finished inserting text, press ESC to end the insert and return to command mode. The dumb terminal now rewrites the line, so that you see all existing text.

Appending Text

a You can append text at any place in your file with the append command a. a works in almost the same way as i, except that text is inserted *after* the cursor rather than *before* the cursor. You may have noticed that when you press i to enter insert mode, the cursor doesn't move until after you enter some text. On the other hand, when you press a to enter insert mode, the cursor moves one space to the right. When you enter text, it appears *after* the original cursor position.

Changing Text

You can replace any text in your file with the change command, c. In order to tell c how much text to change, you combine c with a movement command. In this way, a movement command serves as a *text object* for the c command to affect. For example, c can be used to change text from the cursor:

cw   to the end of a word.

c2b   back two words.

c$ to the end of line.

c0   to the beginning of line.

After issuing a change command, you can replace the identified text with any amount of new text, with no characters at all, with one word, or with hundreds of lines. c, like i and a, leaves you in insert mode until you press the ESC key.

Words

To change a word, combine the c (change) command with w for word. You can replace a word (cw) with a longer or shorter word (or any amount of text). cw can be thought of as "delete the word marked and insert new text until ESC is pressed."

Suppose you have the following line in your file *practice*:

    With an editor you can scroll the page,

and want to change *an* to *a screen*. You need to change only one word.

Keystrokes   **Result**

w

With <u>a</u>n editor you can scroll the page,

Move with w to the place you want the edit to begin.

cw

With <u>a</u>$ editor you can scroll the page,

Give the change word command. The end of the text to be changed will be marked with a $ (dollar sign).

a screen

```
With a scree͟n editor you can scroll the page,
```

Type in the replacement text, and then press ESC to return to command mode.

cw also works on a portion of a word. For example, to change *spelling* to *spelled*, you can position the cursor on the *i*, press cw, then type *ed*.

General Form of vi Commands

In the change commands we've mentioned up to this point, you may have noticed the following pattern:

(command)(*text object*)

command is the change command c, and *text object* is a movement command (you don't type the parentheses). But c is not the only command that requires a text object. The d command (delete) and the y command (yank) follow this pattern as well.

Remember also that movement commands take numeric arguments, so numbers can be added to the text objects of c, d, and y commands. For example, d2w or 2dw is a command to delete two words. With this in mind, you can see that most *vi* commands follow a general pattern:

(command)(*number*)(*text object*)

or the equivalent form:

(number)(*command*)(*text object*)

Here's how this works. *number* and *command* are optional. Without them, you simply have a movement command. If you add a *number*, you have a multiple movement. On the other hand, combine a *command* (c, d, or y) with a *text object* to get an editing command.

When you realize how many combinations are possible in this way, *vi* becomes a powerful editor indeed!

Lines

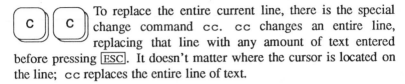

To replace the entire current line, there is the special change command cc. cc changes an entire line, replacing that line with any amount of text entered before pressing ESC. It doesn't matter where the cursor is located on the line; cc replaces the entire line of text.

A command like cw works differently from a command like cc. In using cw, the old text remains until you type over it, and any old text that is left over (up to the $) goes away when you press ESC. In using cc, though, the old text is wiped out first, leaving you a blank line on which to insert text.

The "type over" approach happens with any change command that affects less than a whole line, whereas the "blank line" approach happens with any change command that affects one or more lines.

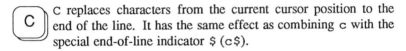

C replaces characters from the current cursor position to the end of the line. It has the same effect as combining c with the special end-of-line indicator $ (c$).

The commands cc and C are really shortcuts for other commands, so they don't follow the general form of *vi* commands. You'll see other shortcuts when we discuss the delete and yank commands.

Characters

One other replacement edit is given by the r command. r replaces a single character with another single character. You do *not* have to press ESC to return to command mode after making the edit.

There is a misspelling in the line below:

```
Pith a screen editor you can scroll the page,
```

Only one letter needs to be corrected. You don't want to use cw in this instance because you would have to retype the entire word. Use r to replace a single character at the cursor:

Keystrokes	**Result**

rW

> W̲ith a screen editor you can scroll the page,

Give the replace command r, followed by the replacement character *W*.

Changing Case

Changing the case of a letter is a special form of replacement. The tilde (˜) command will change a lowercase letter to upper-case, or an uppercase letter to lowercase. Position the cursor on the letter whose case you want to change, and type a ˜. The case of the letter will change, and the cursor will move to the next character. The ˜ is unique among *vi* editing commands because you cannot specify a numeric prefix or text object for it to affect.

If you want to change the case of more than one letter at a time, you must filter the text through a UNIX command like t r, as described in Chapter 7, *Advanced Editing*.

Deleting Text

You can also delete any text in your file with the delete command d. Like the change command, the delete command requires a text object (the amount of text to be operated on). You can delete by word (dw), by line (dd and D), or by other movement commands that you will learn later.

With all deletions, you move to where you want the edit to take place, then give the delete command (d) and the text object, such as w for word.

Words

d w   Suppose you have the following text in the file *practice*:

```
Screen editors are are very popular,
since they allowed you to make
changes as you read through a file.
```

with the cursor positioned as shown. You want to delete one *are* in the first line.

Keystrokes　　　　　　　　　**Result**

2w

```
Screen editors are are very popular,
since they allowed you to make
changes as you read through a file.
```

Move the cursor to where you want the edit to begin (*are*).

dw

```
Screen editors are very popular,
since they allowed you to make
changes as you read through a file.
```

Give the delete word command (dw) to delete the word *are*.

dw deletes a word beginning where the cursor is positioned. Notice that the space following the word is deleted.

dw can also be used to delete a portion of a word. In this example:

```
since they allowed you to make
```

you want to delete the *ed* from the end of *allowed*.

Keystrokes　　　　　　　　　**Result**

dw

```
since they allowyou to make
```

Give the delete word command (dw) to delete the word, beginning with the position of the cursor.

dw always deletes the space before the next word on a line, but we don't want to do that in the previous example. To retain the space between words, use de, which will delete only to the end of a word. Typing dE will delete to the end of a word, including punctuation.

You can also delete backward (db) or to the end or beginning of a line (d$ or d0).

Lines

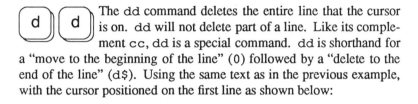

The dd command deletes the entire line that the cursor is on. dd will not delete part of a line. Like its complement cc, dd is a special command. dd is shorthand for a "move to the beginning of the line" (0) followed by a "delete to the end of the line" (d$). Using the same text as in the previous example, with the cursor positioned on the first line as shown below:

```
Screen editors are very popular,
since they allow you to make
changes as you read through a file.
```

you can delete the first two lines:

Keystrokes   **Result**

2dd
```
changes as you read through a file.
```

Give the command to delete two lines (2dd). Note that even though the cursor was not positioned on the beginning of the line, the entire line is deleted.

If you are using a "dumb" terminal, line deletions look different. The dumb terminal will not redraw the screen until you scroll past the bottom of the screen. On a dumb terminal the deletion looks like this:

Keystrokes   **Result**

2dd

```
@
@
changes as you read through a file.
```

Give the command to delete two lines (2dd). An @ symbol "holds the place" of the deleted line, until the terminal redraws the entire screen.

D   The D command deletes from the cursor position to the end of the line. (D is a shortcut for d$.) For example, with the cursor positioned as shown:

```
Screen editors are very popular,
since they allow you to make
changes as you read through a file.
```

you can delete the portion of the line to the right of the cursor.

Keystrokes   **Result**

D

```
Screen editors are very popular,
since they allow you to make
changes
```

Give the command to delete the portion of the line to the right of the cursor (D).

Characters

X   Often you want to delete only one or two characters. Just as r is a special change command to replace a single character, x is a special delete command to delete a single character. x deletes only the character the cursor is on. In the line below:

```
zYou can move text by deleting text and then
```

you can delete the letter z by pressing x. A capital X deletes the character before the cursor. Prefix either of these commands with a number to delete that number of characters. For example, 5x will delete the five characters to the right of the cursor.

Problems with Deletions

√ *You've deleted the wrong text and you want to get it back.*

There are several ways to recover deleted text. If you've just deleted something and you realize you want it back, simply type u to undo the last command (for example, a dd). This works only if you haven't given any further commands, since u only undoes the most recent command.

You can still recover a recent deletion, however, by using the p command, since *vi* saves the last nine deletions in nine numbered deletion buffers. If you know, for example, that the third deletion back is the one you want to restore, type:

        "3p

to "put" the contents of buffer number 3 on the line below the cursor.

This works only for a deleted *line*. Words, or a portion of a line, are not saved in a buffer. If you want to restore a deleted word or line fragment, and u won't work, use the p command by itself. This restores whatever you've last deleted. The next few subsections will talk more about the commands u and p.

Moving Text

In *vi*, you move text by deleting it and then placing that deleted text elsewhere in the file, like a "cut and paste." Each time you delete a text block, that deletion is temporarily saved in a buffer. Move to another position in your file and use the put command (p) to place that text in the new position. You can move any block of text, although moving is more useful with lines than with words.

p The put command (p) puts the text that is in the buffer *after* the cursor position. The uppercase version of the command, P, puts the text *before* the cursor. If you delete one or more lines, p puts the deleted text on a new line(s) below the cursor. If you delete less than an entire line, p puts the deleted text on the current line, after the cursor.

Suppose in your file *practice* you have the text:

```
You can move text by deleting it and then,
like a "cut and paste",
placing the deleted text elsewhere in the file.
each time you delete a text block.
```

and want to move the second line, *like a "cut and paste"*, below the third line. Using delete, you can make this edit.

Keystrokes   **Result**

dd

```
You can move text by deleting it and then,
placing the deleted text elsewhere in the file.
each time you delete a text block.
```

With the cursor on the second line, delete that line. The text is placed in a buffer (reserved memory).

p

```
You can move text by deleting it and then,
placing that deleted text elsewhere in the file.
like a "cut and paste",
each time you delete a text block.
```

Give the put command, p, to restore the deleted line at the next line below the cursor. To finish reordering this sentence, you would also have to change the punctuation (with r) to match the new structure.

NOTE

Once you delete text, you must restore it before the next change command or delete command. If you make another edit that affects the buffer, your deleted text will be lost. You can repeat the put over and over, so long as you don't make a new edit. In Chapter 4, *Beyond the Basics*, you will learn how to save text you delete in a named buffer so you can retrieve it later.

Transposing Two Letters

You can use xp (delete character and put after cursor) to transpose two letters. For example, in the word *mvoe*, the letters *vo* are transposed (reversed). To correct a transposition, place the cursor on *v* and press x, then p. By coincidence, the word *transpose* helps you remember the sequence xp; x stands for *trans*, and p stands for *pose*.

There is no command to transpose words. The section "More Examples of Mapping Keys" in Chapter 7, *Advanced Editing*, discusses a short sequence of commands that transposes two words.

Copying Text

Often you can save editing time (and keystrokes) by copying a part of your file to use in other places. With the two commands y (for yank) and p (for put), you can copy any amount of text and put that copied text in another place in the file. A yank command copies the selected text into a special buffer, where it is held until another yank (or deletion) occurs. You can then place this copy elsewhere in the file with the put command.

As with change and delete, the yank command can be combined with any movement command (yw, y$, 4yy). Yank is most frequently used with a line (or more) of text, because to yank and put a word usually takes longer than simply to insert the word.

The shortcut yy operates on an entire line, just as dd and cc do. But the shortcut Y, for some reason, does not operate the way D and C do. Instead of yanking from the current position to the end of the line, Y yanks the whole line. Y does the same thing as yy.

Suppose you have in your file *practice* the text:

```
With a screen editor you can
scroll the page.
move the cursor.
delete lines.
```

You want to make three complete sentences, beginning each with *With a screen editor you can*. Instead of moving through the file, making this edit over and over, you can use a yank and put to copy the text to be added.

Keystrokes   **Result**

yy

```
With a screen editor you can
scroll the page.
move the cursor.
delete lines.
```

Yank the line of text that you want to copy into the buffer. The cursor can be anywhere on the line you want to yank (or on the beginning line of a series of lines).

2j

```
With a screen editor you can
scroll the page.
move the cursor.
delete lines.
```

Move the cursor to where you want to put the yanked text.

P

```
With a screen editor you can
scroll the page.
With a screen editor you can
move the cursor.
delete lines.
```

Put the yanked text above the cursor line with P.

jp

```
With a screen editor you can
scroll the page.
With a screen editor you can
move the cursor.
With a screen editor you can
delete lines.
```

Move the cursor down a line and put the yanked text below the cursor line with p.

Yanking uses the same buffer as deleting. Each new deletion or yank replaces the previous contents of the yank buffer. As we'll see in Chapter 4, *Beyond the Basics*, up to nine previous yanks or deletions can be recalled with put commands. You can also yank or delete directly into up to 26 named buffers, which allows you to juggle multiple text blocks at once.

Repeating or Undoing Your Last Command

Each edit command that you give is stored in a temporary buffer until you give the next command. If you insert *the* after a word in your file, the command used to insert the text, along with the text that you entered, is temporarily saved.

Repeat

Any time you make the same editing command over and over, you can save time by duplicating it with the repeat command, the period (.). Position the cursor where you want to repeat the editing command, and type a period.

Suppose you have the following lines in your file *practice*:

```
With a screen editor you can
scroll the page.
With a screen editor you can
move the cursor.
```

You can delete one line, and then, to delete another line, simply type a period.

Keystrokes   **Result**

dd

```
With a screen editor you can
scroll the page.
move the cursor.
```

Delete a line with the command dd.

```
With a screen editor you can
scroll the page.
```

Repeats the deletion.

Occasionally, *vi* has problems repeating a command. For example, it may have difficulty repeating a long insertion when `wrapmargin` is set. This is a bug in *vi* that will probably bite you sooner or later. There's not a lot you can do about it after the fact, but it helps to be forewarned. There are two ways you can guard against a potential problem when repeating long insertions. You can write your file (`:w`) before repeating the insertion (returning to this copy if the insertion doesn't work correctly). You can also turn off `wrapmargin` like this:

```
:set wm=0
```

In Chapter 7, *Advanced Editing*, we'll show you an easy way to use the wrapmargin solution, in the section "More Examples of Mapping Keys." In some versions of *vi*, the command CTRL-@ repeats the last insert (append, etc.) command. CTRL-@ does not repeat deletions.

Undo

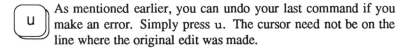

As mentioned earlier, you can undo your last command if you make an error. Simply press u. The cursor need not be on the line where the original edit was made.

To continue the example above, showing deletion of lines in the file *practice*:

Keystrokes   **Result**

u

> With a screen editor you can
> scroll the page.
> move the cursor.

u undoes the last command and restores the deleted line.

U, the uppercase version of u, undoes all edits on a single line, *as long as the cursor remains on that line*. Once you move off a line, you can no longer use U.

Note that you can undo your last undo with u, toggling between two versions of text. u will also undo U, and U will undo any changes to a line, including those made with u. (A tip: the fact that u can undo itself leads to a nifty way to get around in a file. If you ever want to get back to the site of your last edit, simply undo it. You will pop back to the appropriate line. When you undo the undo, you'll stay on that line.)

More Ways to Insert Text

You have inserted text before the cursor with the sequence:

```
itext to be inserted ESC
```

You've also inserted text after the cursor with the a command. There are other insert commands for inserting text at different positions relative to the cursor:

A   Append text to end of current line.
I   Insert text at beginning of line.
o   Open blank line below cursor for text.
O   Open blank line above cursor for text.
s   Delete character at cursor and substitute text.
S   Delete line and substitute text.
R   Overstrike existing characters with new characters.

All of these commands leave you in insert mode. After inserting text, remember to press ESC to escape back to command mode.

A (append) and I (insert) save you from having to move your cursor to the end or beginning of the line before invoking insert mode. (The A command saves one keystroke over $a. Although one keystroke might not seem like much of a saving, the more adept (and impatient) an editor you become, the more keystrokes you will want to omit.)

o and O (open) save you from having to insert a carriage return. You can type these commands from anywhere within the line.

s and S (substitute) allow you to delete a character or a whole line and replace the deletion with any amount of new text. s is the equivalent of the two-stroke command c SPACE, and S is the same as cc. One of the best uses for s is to change one character to several characters.

R ("large" replace) is useful when you want to start changing text, but you don't know exactly how much. For example, instead of guessing whether to say 3cw or 4cw, just type R and then enter your replacement text.

Numeric Arguments for Insert Commands

Except for o and O, the above insert commands (plus i and a) take numeric prefixes. With numeric prefixes, you might use the commands i, I, a, and A to insert a row of underlines or alternating characters. For example, typing 50i*[ESC] inserts 50 asterisks, and typing 25a*-[ESC] appends 50 characters (25 pairs of asterisk and hyphen). It's better to repeat only a small string of characters. *vi* has difficulty repeating the insertion of more than one line's worth of text.

You can use a numeric prefix with S to substitute several lines. It's quicker and more flexible, though, to use c with a movement command.

A good case for using the s command with a numeric prefix is when you want to change a few characters in the middle of a word. Typing r wouldn't be enough, but typing cw would change too much text. Using s with a numeric prefix is usually the same as typing R.

There are other combinations of commands that work naturally together. For example, ea is useful for appending new text to the end of a word. It helps to train yourself to recognize such frequent combinations so that they become automatic.

Joining Two Lines with J

J | Sometimes while editing a file you will end up with a series of short lines that are difficult to scan. When you want to merge two lines into one, position the cursor anywhere on the first line, and press J to join the two lines.

Suppose your file *practice* reads:

```
With a
screen editor
you can
scroll the page, move the cursor
```

Keystrokes	Result

J

```
With a screen editor
you can
scroll the page, move the cursor
```

J joins the line the cursor is on with the line below.

```
With a screen editor you can
scroll the page, move the cursor
```

Repeat the last command (J) with the . to join the next line with the current line.

Using a numeric argument with J joins that number of consecutive lines. In the example above, you could also have used the command 2J.

Problem Checklist

√ *When you type commands, text jumps around on the screen and nothing works the way it's supposed to.*

You may have hit the CAPS LOCK key without noticing it. *vi* is case-sensitive. That is, uppercase commands (I, A, J, etc.) are different from lowercase commands (i, a, j), so all your commands are being interpreted not as lowercase but as uppercase commands. Press the CAPS LOCK key again to return to lowercase, then type either U to restore the last line changed or u to undo the last command. You'll probably also have to do some additional editing to fully restore the garbled part of your file.

Review of Basic vi Commands

Table 2-1 presents a few of the commands you can perform by combining the commands c, d, and y with various text objects. The last two rows show additional commands for editing. Table 2-2 lists some other basic commands.

Table 2-1: Edit Commands

Text Object	Change	Delete	Copy
1 word	cw	dw	yw
2 words, not counting punctuation	2cW or c2W	2dW or d2W	2yW or y2W
3 words back	3cb or c3b	3db or d3b	3yb or y3b
1 line	cc	dd	yy or Y
to end of line	c$ or C	d$ or D	y$
to beginning of line	c0	d0	y0
single character	r	x or X	y1 or yh
five characters	5s	5x	5y1

Table 2-2: Movement and Other Commands

Movement	Commands
←,↓,↑,→	h, j, k, l
forward by word	w or W
backward by word	b or B
to end of line	$
to beginning of line	0
Other Operations	
place text from buffer	P or p
start *vi*, open file if specified	vi *file*
save edits, quit file	ZZ
no saving of edits, quit file	:q!

You can get by in *vi* using only the commands listed in Table 2-1 and Table 2-2. However, in order to harness the real power of *vi* (and increase your own productivity), you will need more tools. The following chapters describe those tools.

3

Moving Around in a Hurry

Movement by Screens
Movement by Text Blocks
Movement by Searches
Movement by Line Number

You will not use *vi* only to create new files. You'll spend a lot of your time in *vi* editing existing files. You rarely want to simply open to the first line in the file and move through it line by line. You want to get to a specific place in a file and start work.

All edits begin by moving the cursor to where you want to begin the edit (or, with *ex* line editor commands, by identifying the line numbers to be edited). This chapter shows you how to think about movement in a variety of ways (by screens, by text, by patterns, or by line numbers). There are many ways to move in *vi*, since editing speed depends on getting to your destination with only a few keystrokes.

This chapter covers:

☐ Movement by screens.

☐ Movement by text blocks.

☐ Movement by searches for patterns.

☐ Movement by line number.

Movement by Screens

When you read a book, you think of "places" in the book by page: the page where you stopped reading or the page number in an index. You don't have this convenience when you're editing files. Some *vi* files take up only a few lines, and you can see the whole file at once. But many files have hundreds of lines.

You can think of a *vi* file as text on a long roll of paper. The screen is a window of (usually) 24 lines of text on that long roll.

In insert mode, as you fill up the screen with text, you will end up typing on the bottom line of the screen. When you reach the end and press [RETURN], the top line rolls out of sight, and a blank line appears on the bottom of the screen for new text. This is called scrolling.

In command mode, you can move through a file to see any text in it by scrolling the screen ahead or back. And, since cursor movements can be multiplied by numeric prefixes, you can move quickly to anywhere in your file.

Scrolling the Screen

 There are *vi* commands to scroll forward and backward through the file by full and half screens:

    ^F   Scroll forward one screen.
    ^B   Scroll backward one screen.
    ^D   Scroll forward half screen (down).
    ^U   Scroll backward half screen (up).

(In the list of commands above, the ^ symbol represents the CTRL key. ^F means to hold down the CTRL key and press the f key simultaneously.)

There are also commands to scroll the screen up one line (^E) and down one line (^Y). However, these two commands do not send the cursor to the beginning of the line. The cursor remains at the same point in the line as when the command was issued. (These commands are not available on small systems, such as the PDP-11 or Xenix for the PC-XT.)

Scrolling with z

If you want to scroll the screen up or down, but you want the cursor to remain on the line where you left it, use the z command.

z RETURN   Move current line to top of screen and scroll.
z .   Move current line to center of screen and scroll.
z -   Move current line to bottom of screen and scroll.

With the z command, using a numeric prefix as a multiplier makes no sense. (After all, you would need to reposition the cursor to the top of the screen only once. Repeating the same z command wouldn't move anything.) Instead, z understands a numeric prefix as a line number that it will use in place of the current line. For example, z RETURN moves the current line to the top of the screen, but 200z RETURN moves line 200 to the top of the screen.

Redrawing the Screen

Sometimes while you're editing, messages from your computer system will display on your screen. These messages don't become part of your editing buffer, but they do interfere with your work. When system messages appear on your screen, you need to redisplay, or redraw, the screen.

Whenever you scroll, you redraw part of (or all of) the screen, so you can always get rid of unwanted messages by scrolling them off the screen and then returning to your previous position. But you can also redraw the screen without scrolling, by typing either CTRL-L or CTRL-R, depending on your terminal type.

Movement Within a Screen

 You can also keep your current screen, or view of the file, and move around within the screen using:

H   Move to home – top line on screen.
M   Move to middle line on screen.
L   Move to last line on screen.
nH   Move to n lines below top line.
nL   Move to n lines above last line.

H moves the cursor from anywhere on the screen to the first, or "home," line. M moves to the middle line, L to the last. To move to the line below the first line, use 2H.

Keystrokes   **Result**

L
```
With a screen editor you can
scroll the page, move the cursor,
delete lines, insert characters, and more,
while seeing the results of your
edits as you make them.
Screen editors are very popular,
since they allow you to make changes
as you read through a file.
```
Move to the last line of the screen with the L command.

2H
```
With a screen editor you can
scroll the page, move the cursor,
delete lines, insert characters, and more,
while seeing the results of your
edits as you make them.
Screen editors are very popular,
since they allow you to make changes
as you read through a file.
```
Move to the second line of the screen with the 2H command. (H alone moves to the top line of the screen.)

Movement by Line

RETURN

Within the current screen there are also commands to move by line. You've already seen j and k. You can also use:

RETURN	Move to first character of next line.
+	Move to first character of next line.
−	Move to first character of previous line.

The above three commands move down or up to the first *character* of the line, ignoring any spaces or tabs. j and k, by contrast, move the cursor down or up to the first position of a line, even if that position is blank (and assuming that the cursor started at the first position).

Movement on the Current Line

Don't forget that h and l move the cursor to the left and right and that 0 and $ move the cursor to the beginning or end of the line. You can also use:

^	Move to first character of current line.
n |	Move to column *n* of current line.

As with the line movement commands above, ^ moves to the first *character* of the line, ignoring any spaces or tabs. 0, by contrast, moves to the first position of the line, even if that position is blank.

Movement by Text Blocks

e

Another way that you can think of moving through a *vi* file is by text blocks—words, sentences, paragraphs, or sections. You have already learned to move forward and backward by word (w, W, b or B). In addition, you can use these commands:

e	Move to end of word.
E	Move to end of word (ignore punctuation).
(	Move to beginning of previous sentence.
)	Move to beginning of next sentence.

{	Move to beginning of previous paragraph.
}	Move to beginning of next paragraph.
[[	Move to beginning of previous section.
]]	Move to beginning of next section.

To find the end of a sentence, *vi* looks for one of the punctuation marks ? . !. *vi* locates the end of a sentence when the punctuation is followed by at least two spaces or when it appears as the last nonblank character on a line. If you have left only a single space following a period, or if the sentence ends with a quotation mark, *vi* won't recognize the sentence.

A paragraph is defined as text up to the next blank line, or up to one of the default paragraph macros (.IP, .PP, .LP, or .QP) from the *nroff/troff* ms macro package. Similarly, a section is defined as text up to the next default section macro (.NH, .SH, .H 1, .HU). The macros that are recognized as paragraph or section separators can be customized with the : set command, as described in Chapter 7, *Advanced Editing*.

Remember that you can combine numbers with movement. For example, 3) moves ahead three sentences. Also remember that you can edit using movement commands: d) deletes to the end of the current sentence, 2y} copies (yanks) two paragraphs ahead.

▓ Movement by Searches

One of the most useful ways to move around in a large file quickly is by searching for text, or more properly, a *pattern* of characters. Sometimes a search can be performed to find a misspelled word or to find each occurrence of a variable in a program.

The search command is the special character / (slash). When you enter a slash, it appears on the bottom line of the screen; then type in the *pattern* that you want to find:

```
/pattern
```

A pattern can be a whole word or any other sequence of characters (called a "character string"). For example, if you search for the characters *red*, you will match "*red*" as a whole word, but you'll also match "occur*red*". If you include a space before or after *pattern*, the spaces will be treated as part of the word. As with all bottom-line commands, press RETURN to finish. (*vi*, like all other UNIX editors, has a special pattern-matching language that allows you to look for variable text patterns; for example, any word beginning with a capital letter, or the word *The* at the beginning of a line.) We'll talk about this more powerful pattern-matching syntax in Chapter 6, *Global Replacement*. For right now, think of *pattern* simply as a word or phrase.)

vi begins the search at the cursor and searches forward, wrapping around to the start of the file if necessary. The cursor will move to the first occurrence of the pattern. If there is no match, the message "Pattern not found" will be shown on the status line.

Using the file *practice*, here's how to move the cursor by searches:

Keystrokes	Result
/edits	

> With a screen editor you can scroll the
> page, move the cursor, delete lines, insert
> characters, and more, while seeing the
> results of your edits as you make them.

Search for the pattern *edits*. Press RETURN to enter. The cursor moves directly to that pattern.

/scr

> With a screen editor you can scroll the
> page, move the cursor, delete lines, insert
> characters, and more, while seeing the
> results of your edits as you make them.

Search for the pattern *scr*. Press RETURN to enter. Note that there is no space after *scr*.

The search wraps around to the front of the file. Note that you can give any combination of characters; a search does not have to be for a complete word.

To begin a search backward, type a ? instead of a /:

    ?pattern

In this case, the search wraps around to the end of the file, if necessary.

Repeating Searches

⊓ The last pattern that you searched for stays available throughout your editing session. After a search, instead of repeating your original keystrokes, you can use a command to search again for the last pattern.

n	Repeat search in same direction.
N	Repeat search in opposite direction.
/ [RETURN]	Repeat search forward.
? [RETURN]	Repeat search backward.

Since the last pattern stays available, you can search for a pattern, do some work, and then search again for the same pattern without retyping it by using n, N, / or ?. The direction of your search (/ is forward, ? is backward) is displayed at the bottom left of the screen.

To continue with the example above, since the pattern *scr* is still available for search, you can:

Keystrokes   **Result**

n

```
With a screen editor you can scroll the
page, move the cursor, delete lines, insert
characters, and more, while seeing the
results of your edits as you make them.
```

Move to the next instance of the pattern *scr* (from *screen* to *scroll*) with the n (next) command.

?you

```
With a screen editor you can scroll the
page, move the cursor, delete lines, insert
characters, and more, while seeing the
results of your edits as you make them.
```

Search backward with ? from the cursor to the first occurrence of *you*. You need to press RETURN after typing the pattern.

N

> With a screen editor you can scroll the
> page, move the cursor, delete lines, insert
> characters, and more, while seeing the
> results of your edits as you make them.

Repeat previous search for *you* but in the opposite direction (forward).

Sometimes you want to find a word only if it is further ahead; you don't want the search to wrap around earlier in the file. *vi* has an option, `wrapscan`, that controls whether searches wrap. You can disable wrapping like this:

```
:set nowrapscan
```

When `nowrapscan` is set and a forward search fails, the status line displays the message:

```
Address search hit BOTTOM without matching pattern
```

When `nowrapscan` is set and a backward search fails, the message displays "TOP" instead of "BOTTOM".

This section has given only the barest introduction to searching for patterns. Chapter 6, *Global Replacement*, will teach more about pattern matching and its use in making global changes to a file.

Current Line Searches

There are also miniature versions of the search commands that operate within the current line. The command `fx` moves the cursor to the next instance of the character *x* (where *x* stands for any character). The command `tx` moves the cursor to the character *before* the next instance of *x*. Semicolons can then be used repeatedly to "find" your way along.

The in-line search commands are summarized below. None of these commands will move the cursor to the next line.

    `fx`   Find (move cursor to) next occurrence of *x* in the line, where *x* stands for any character.

    `Fx`   Find (move cursor to) previous occurrence of *x* in the line.

t*x*   Find (move cursor to) character *before* next occurrence of *x* in the line.

T*x*   Find (move cursor to) character *after* previous occurrence of *x* in the line.

;   Repeat previous find command in same direction.

,   Repeat previous find command in opposite direction.

With any of these commands, a numeric prefix *n* will locate the *n*th occurrence. Suppose you are editing in *practice*, on this line:

```
With a screen editor you can scroll the
```

Keystrokes   **Result**

fo

```
With a screen editor you can scroll the
```

Find the first occurrence of *o* in your current line with f .

;

```
With a screen editor you can scroll the
```

Move to the next occurrence of *o* with the ; command (find next *o*).

d f*x* deletes up to and including the named character *x*. This command is useful in deleting or yanking partial lines. You might need to use d f*x* instead of dw if there were symbols or punctuation within the line that made counting words difficult. The t command works just like f, except that it positions the cursor before the character searched for. For example, the command ct . could be used to change text up to the end of a sentence, leaving the period.

Movement by Line Number

A file contains sequentially numbered lines, and you can move through a file by specifying line numbers.

Line numbers are useful for identifying the beginning and end of large blocks of text you want to edit. Line numbers are also useful for programmers, since compiler error messages refer to line numbers.

Line numbers are also used by *ex* commands, which you will learn in the next chapters.

If you are going to move by line numbers, you must have a way to identify them. Line numbers can be displayed on the screen using the :set nu option described in Chapter 7, *Advanced Editing*. In *vi*, you can also display the current line number on the bottom of the screen.

The command CTRL-G causes the following to be displayed at the bottom of your screen: the current line number, the total number of lines in the file, and what percentage of the total the present line number represents. For example, for the file *practice*, CTRL-G might display:

```
"practice" line 3 of 6 --50%--
```

CTRL-G is useful either for displaying the line number to use in a command or for orienting yourself if you have been distracted from your editing session.

The G (Go To) Command

G   You can use line numbers to move the cursor through a file. The G (go to) command uses a line number as a numeric argument and moves directly to that line. For instance, 44G moves the cursor to the beginning of line 44. G without a line number moves the cursor to the last line of the file.

Typing two backquotes (' ') returns you to your original position (the position where you issued the last G command), unless you have done some edits in the meantime. If you have made an edit, and then moved the cursor using some command other than G, ' ' will return the cursor to the site of your last edit. If you have issued a search command (/ or ?), ' ' will return the cursor to its position when you started the search. A pair of apostrophes (' ') works much like two backquotes, except that it returns the cursor to the beginning of the line instead of the exact position on that line where your cursor had been.

The total number of lines shown with CTRL-G can be used to give yourself a rough idea of how many lines to move. If you are on line 10 of a 1,000 line file:

```
"practice" line 10 of 1000 --1%--
```

and know that you want to begin editing near the end of that file, you could give an approximation of your destination with:

```
800G
```

Movement by line number is a tool that can move you quickly from place to place through a large file.

4

Beyond the Basics
More Command Combinations
Options When Starting vi
Making Use of Buffers
Marking Your Place
Other Advanced Edits

You have already been introduced to the basic *vi* editing commands, i, a, c, d, and y. This chapter expands on what you already know about editing. It covers:

☐ Review of general command form.

☐ Additional ways to enter *vi*.

☐ Making use of buffers that store yanks and deletions.

☐ Marking your place in a file.

More Command Combinations

In Chapter 2, *Simple Editing*, you learned the edit commands c, d, and y, as well as how to combine them with movements and numbers (such as 2cw or 4dd). In Chapter 3, *Moving Around in a Hurry*, you added many more movement commands to your repertoire. Although the fact that you can combine edit commands with movement is not a new concept to you, Table 4-1 gives you a feel for the many editing options you now have.

Table 4-1: More Editing Commands

Change	Delete	Copy	from Cursor to ...
cH	dH	yH	top of screen
cL	dL	yL	bottom of screen
c+	d+	y+	next line
c5 |	d5 |	y5 |	column 5 of current line
2c)	2d)	2y)	second sentence following
c{	d{	y{	previous paragraph
c/*pattern*	d/*pattern*	y/*pattern*	*pattern*
cn	dn	yn	next *pattern*
cG	dG	yG	end of file
c13G	d13G	y13G	line number 13

Notice how all of the above sequences follow the general pattern:

(number)(command)(text object)

number is the optional numeric argument. *command* in this case is one of c, d, or y. *text object* is a movement command.

The general form of a *vi* command is discussed in Chapter 2. You may wish to review Table 2-1 and Table 2-2 as well.

Options When Starting vi

In this handbook, you have invoked the *vi* editor with the command:

    $ vi file

There are other options to the `vi` command that can be helpful. You can open a file directly to a specific line number or pattern. You can also open a file in read-only mode. Another option recovers all changes to a file that you were editing when the system crashed.

Advancing to a Specific Place

When you begin editing an existing file, you can call the file in and then move to the first occurrence of a *pattern* or to a specific line number. You can also specify your first movement by search or by line number right on the command line:

`$ vi +n file`	Opens *file* at line number *n*.
`$ vi + file`	Opens *file* at last line.
`$ vi +/pattern file`	Opens *file* at the first occurrence of *pattern*.

In the file *practice*, to open the file and advance directly to the line containing the word *Screen*, enter:

Keystrokes   **Result**

`vi +/Screen practice`

```
With a screen editor you can scroll
the page, move the cursor, delete
lines, and insert characters, while
seeing the results of your edits as
you make them.
Screen editors are
very popular, since they allow you
to make changes as you read
```

Give the `vi` command with the option *+/pattern* to go directly to the line containing *Screen*.

As you see in the example above, your search pattern will not necessarily be positioned at the top of the screen.

If you include spaces in the *pattern*, you must enclose the whole pattern within single or double quotes:

```
+/"you make"
```

or escape the space with a backslash:

```
+/you\ make
```

In addition, if you want to use the general pattern-matching syntax described in Chapter 6, *Global Replacement*, you may need to protect one or more special characters from interpretation by the shell with either single quotes or backslashes.

Using *+/pattern* is helpful if you have to leave an editing session in the middle. You can mark your place by inserting a pattern such as ZZZ or HERE. Then when you return to the file, all you have to remember is /ZZZ or /HERE.

NOTE

Normally, when you're editing in *vi*, the wrapscan option is enabled. If you've customized your environment so that wrapscan is always disabled, you might not be able to use *+/pattern*. If you try to open a file this way, *vi* opens the file at the last line and displays the message "Address search hit BOTTOM without matching pattern."

Read-only Mode

There will be times when you want to look at a file but want to protect that file from inadvertent keystrokes and changes. (You might want to call in a lengthy file to practice *vi* movements, or you might want to scroll through a command file or program). You can enter a file in read-only mode and use all the *vi* movement commands, but you won't be able to change the file.

To look at a file in read-only mode, enter either:

```
$ vi -R file
```

or:

```
$ view file
```

(The `view` command, like the `vi` command, can use any of the command-line options for advancing to a specific place in the file.) If you do decide to make some edits to the file, you can override read-only mode by adding an exclamation point to the `write` command:

```
:w!
```

or:

```
:wq!
```

If you have a problem writing out the file, see the problem checklists summarized in Appendix D, *Problem Checklist*.

Recovering a Buffer

Occasionally there is a system failure while you are editing a file. Ordinarily, any edits made after your last write (save) are lost. However, there is an option, -r, which lets you recover the edited buffer at the time of a system crash.

When you first log on after the system is running again, you will receive a mail message stating that your buffer has been saved.

In addition, if you type the command:

```
$ ex -r
```

or:

```
$ vi -r
```

you will get a list of any files that the system has saved.

Use the −r option with a file name to recover the edited buffer. For example, to recover the edited buffer of the file *practice* after a system crash, enter:

```
$ vi -r practice
```

It is wise to recover the file immediately, lest you inadvertently make edits to the file, and then have to resolve a version skew between the preserved buffer and the newly edited file.

You can force the system to preserve your buffer even when there is not a crash by using the command :pre. You may find it useful if you have made edits to a file, then discover that you can't save your edits because you don't have write permission. (You could also just write a copy of the file out under another name or into a directory where you do have write permission. See the section "Problems Saving Files" in Chapter 1, *The vi Text Editor*.)

Making Use of Buffers

You have seen that while you are editing, your last deletion (d or x) or yank (y) is saved in a buffer (a place in stored memory). You can access the contents of that buffer and put the saved text back in your file with the put command (p or P).

The last nine deletions are stored by *vi* in numbered buffers. You can access any of these numbered buffers to restore any (or all) of the last nine deletions. (Small deletions, of only parts of lines, are not saved in numbered buffers, however.) These deletions can only be recovered by using the p or P command immediately after you've made the deletion.

vi also allows you to place yanks (copied text) in buffers identified by letters. You can fill up to 26 (a-z) buffers with yanked text and restore that text with a put command at any time in your editing session.

Recovering Deletions

Being able to delete large blocks of text at a single bound is all very well and good, but what if you mistakenly delete 53 lines that you need? There is a way to recover any of your past *nine* deletions, for they are saved in numbered buffers. The last delete is saved in buffer 1, the second-to-last in buffer 2, and so on.

To recover a deletion, type " (double quote), identify the buffered text by number, then give the put command. To recover your second-to-last deletion from buffer 2, type:

    "2p

The deletion in buffer 2 is placed after the cursor.

If you're not sure which buffer contains the deletion you want to restore, you don't have to keep typing "*n*p over and over again. If you use the repeat command (.) with p after u, it automatically increments the buffer number. As a result, you can search through the numbered buffers as follows:

    "1pu.u.u *etc.*

to put the contents of each succeeding buffer in the file one after the other. Each time you type u, the restored text is removed; when you type a dot (.), the contents of the *next* buffer is restored to your file. Keep typing u and . until you've recovered the text you're looking for.

Yanking to Named Buffers

You have seen that you must "put" (p or P) the contents of an unnamed buffer before you make any other edit, or the buffer will be overwritten. You can also use y and d with a set of 26 named buffers (a-z) which are specifically available for copying and moving text. If you name a buffer to store the yanked text, you can place the contents of the named buffer at any time during your editing session.

To yank into a named buffer, precede the yank command with a double quote (") and the character for the name of the buffer you want to load. For example:

    "dyy   Yank current line into buffer d.
    "a7yy   Yank next seven lines into buffer a.

After loading the named buffers and moving to the new position, use p or P to put the text back:

`"dP`	Put the contents of buffer d before cursor.
`"ap`	Put the contents of buffer a after cursor.

There is no way to put part of a buffer into the text—it is all or nothing.

In the next chapter, you'll learn to edit multiple files. Once you know how to travel between files without leaving *vi*, you can use named buffers to selectively transfer text between files.

You can also delete text into named buffers using much the same procedure. For example:

`"a5dd`	Delete five lines into buffer a.

If you specify a buffer name with a capital letter, your yanked or deleted text will be appended to the current contents of that buffer. This allows you to be selective in what you move or copy. For example:

`"zd)`	Delete from cursor to end of current sentence and save in buffer z.
`2)`	Move two sentences further on.
`"Zy)`	Add the next sentence to buffer z.

Note that you can continue adding more text to a named buffer for as long as you like—but be warned: if you once forget, and yank or delete to the buffer without specifying its name in capitalized form, you'll overwrite the buffer, losing whatever you previously accumulated in it.

Marking Your Place

During a *vi* session, you can mark your place in the file with an invisible "bookmark," perform edits elsewhere, then return to your marked place. In command mode:

m*x*	Marks current position with *x* (*x* can be any letter).
'*x*	(apostrophe) Moves cursor to first character of line marked by *x*.
`*x*	(backquote) Moves cursor to character marked by *x*.
` `	(backquotes) Returns to exact position of previous mark or context after a move.
' '	(apostrophes) Returns to the beginning of the line of the previous mark or context.

Place markers are set only during the current *vi* session; they are not stored in the file.

Other Advanced Edits

There are other advanced edits that you can execute with *vi*, but to use them you must first learn a bit more about the *ex* editor by reading the next chapter.

5

Introducing the ex Editor

ex Commands
Editing with ex
Saving and Exiting Files
Copying a File into Another File
Editing Multiple Files

If this is a handbook on *vi*, why would we include a chapter on another editor? *ex* is not really another editor. *vi* is the visual mode of the more general, underlying line editor, *ex*. Some *ex* commands can be useful to you while you are working in *vi*, for they can save you a lot of editing time. Most of these commands can be used without ever leaving *vi*.

You already know how to think of files as a sequence of numbered lines. *ex* simply gives you editing commands with greater mobility and scope. With *ex* you can move easily between files and transfer text from one file to another in a variety of ways. You can quickly edit blocks of text larger than a single screen. And with global replacement you can make substitutions throughout a file for a given pattern.

This chapter introduces *ex* and its commands. You will learn how to:

☐ Move around a file by using line numbers.

☐ Use *ex* commands to copy, move, and delete blocks of text.

☐ Save files and parts of files.

☐ Work with multiple files (reading in text or commands, traveling between files).

ex Commands

Long before *vi* or any other screen editor was invented, people communicated with computers on printing terminals, rather than on today's CRTs. Line numbers were a way to quickly identify a part of a file to be worked on, and line editors evolved to edit those files. A programmer or other computer user would typically print out a line (or lines) on the printing terminal, give the editing commands to change just that line, then reprint to check the edited line.

People rarely edit files on printing terminals any more, but some *ex* line editor commands are still useful to users of the more sophisticated visual editor built on top of *ex*. Although it is simpler to make most edits with *vi*, the line orientation of *ex* gives it an advantage when you want to make large-scale changes to more than one part of a file.

Before you start off simply memorizing *ex* commands (or worse, ignoring them), let's first take some of the mystery out of line editors. Seeing how *ex* works when it is invoked directly will help make sense of the sometimes obscure command syntax.

Open a file that is familiar to you and try a few *ex* commands. Just as you can invoke the *vi* editor on a file, you can invoke the *ex* line editor on a file. If you invoke *ex*, you will see a message about the total number of lines in the file, and a colon command prompt.

For example:

```
$ ex practice
"practice" 6 lines, 320 characters
:
```

You won't see any lines in the file unless you give an *ex* command that causes one or more lines to be displayed.

ex commands consist of a line address (which can simply be a line number) plus a command; they are finished with a carriage return. One of the most basic commands is p for print (to the screen). So, for example, if you type 1p at the prompt, you will see the first line of the file:

```
:1p
With a screen editor you can
:
```

In fact, you can leave off the p, because a line number by itself is equivalent to a print command for that line. To print more than one line, you can specify a range of line numbers (for example, 1, 3—two numbers separated by commas, with or without spaces in between). For example:

```
:1,3
With a screen editor you can
scroll the page, move the cursor,
delete lines, insert characters, and more,
```

A command without a line number is assumed to affect the current line. So, for example, the substitute command (s), which allows you to substitute one word for another, could be entered like this:

```
:1
With a screen editor you can
:s/screen/line/
With a line editor you can
```

Notice that the changed line is reprinted after the command is issued. You could also make the same change like this:

```
:1s/screen/line/
With a line editor you can
```

Even though you will be invoking *ex* commands from *vi* and will not be using them directly, it is worthwhile to spend a few minutes in *ex* itself. You will get a feel for how you need to tell the editor which line (or lines) to work on, as well as which command to execute.

After you have given a few *ex* commands on your *practice* file, you should invoke *vi* on that same file, so that you can see it in the more familiar visual mode. The command :vi will get you from *ex* to *vi*.

To invoke an *ex* command from *vi*, you must type the special bottom line character : (colon). Then type the command and press [RETURN] to execute it. So, for example, in the *ex* editor you move to a line simply by typing the number of the line at the colon prompt. To move to line 6 of a file using this command from within *vi*, enter:

    : 6

Press [RETURN].

Following the exercise, we will be discussing *ex* commands only as they are executed from *vi*.

Exercise: The *ex* Editor

At the UNIX prompt, invoke ex editor on a practice file	`ex practice`
A message appears	`"practice"  6 lines 320 characters`
Go to and print (display) first line	`:1`
Print (display) lines 1 through 3	`:1,3`
Substitute screen for line on line 1	`:1s/screen/line`
Invoke vi editor on file	`:vi`
Go to first line	`:1`

Problem Checklist

√ *While editing in vi, you accidentally end up in the ex editor.*

A Q in the command mode of *vi* invokes *ex*. Any time you are in *ex*, the command : v i returns you to the *vi* editor.

Editing with ex

Many *ex* commands that perform normal editing operations have an equivalent in *vi* that does the job more simply. Obviously, you will use dw or dd to delete a single word or line rather than using the `delete` command in *ex*. However, when you want to make changes that affect numerous lines, you will find the *ex* commands more useful. They allow you to modify large blocks of text with a single command.

These *ex* commands are listed below, along with abbreviations for those commands. Remember that in *vi* each *ex* command must be preceded with a colon. You can use the full command name or the abbreviation, whichever is easier to remember.

`delete`	d	Delete lines.
`move`	m	Move lines.
`copy`	co	Copy lines.
	t	Copy lines (a synonym for co).

You can separate the different elements of an *ex* command with spaces, if you find the command easier to read that way. For example, you can separate line addresses, patterns, and commands in this way. You cannot, however, use a space as a separator inside a pattern or at the end of a substitute command.

Line Addresses

For each *ex* editing command, you have to tell *ex* which line number(s) to edit. And for the *ex* move and copy commands, you also need to tell *ex* where to move or copy the text to.

You can specify line addresses in several ways:

- With explicit line numbers.
- With symbols that help you to specify line numbers relative to your current position in the file.
- With search patterns as *addresses* that identify the lines to be affected.

Let's look at some examples.

Defining a Range of Lines

You can use line numbers to define explicitly a line or range of lines. Addresses that use explicit numbers are called *absolute* line addresses. For example:

:3,18d	Delete lines 3 through 18.
:160,224m23	Move lines 160 through 244 to follow line 23. (Like delete and put in *vi*.)
:23,29co100	Copy lines 23 through 29 and put after line 100. (Like yank and put in *vi*.)

To make editing with line numbers easier, you can also display all line numbers on the left of the screen. The command:

```
:set number
```

or its abbreviation:

```
:set nu
```

displays line numbers. The file *practice* then appears:

```
1  With a screen editor
2  you can scroll the page,
3  move the cursor, delete lines,
4  insert characters and more
```

The displayed line numbers are not saved when you write a file, and they do not print if you print the file. Line numbers are displayed either until you quit the *vi* session or until you disable the *set* option:

```
:set nonumber
```

or:

```
:set nonu
```

To temporarily display the line numbers for a set of lines, you can use the # sign. For example:

```
:1,10#
```

would display the line numbers from line one to line ten.

As described in Chapter 3, *Moving Around in a Hurry*, you can also use the CTRL-G command to display the current line number. You can thus identify the line numbers corresponding to the start and end of a block of text by moving to the start of the block, typing CTRL-G, then moving to the end of the block and typing CTRL-G again.

Yet another way to identify line numbers is with the *ex* = command:

`:=`	Print the total number of lines.
`:.=`	Print the line number of the current line.
`:/pattern/=`	Print the line number of the first line that matches *pattern*.

Line Addressing Symbols

You can also use symbols for line addresses. A dot (.) stands for the current line; $ stands for the last line of the file. % stands for every line in the file; it's the same as the combination 1, $. These symbols can also be combined with absolute line addresses. For example:

`:.,$d`	Delete from current line to end of file.
`:20,.m$`	Move from line 20 through the current line to the end of the file.
`:%d`	Delete all the lines in a file.
`:%t$`	Copy all lines and place them at the end of the file (making a consecutive duplicate).

In addition to an absolute line address, you can specify an address relative to the current line. The symbols + and − work like arithmetic operators. When placed before a number, these symbols add or subtract the value that follow. For example:

`:.,.+20d`	Delete from current line through the next 20 lines.
`:226,$m.-2`	Move lines 226 through the end of the file to two lines above the current line.
`:.,+20#`	Display line numbers from the current line to 20 lines further on in the file.

In fact, you don't need to type the dot (.) when you use + or −, because the current line is the assumed starting position.

Without a number following them, + and − are equivalent to +1 and −1, respectively.* Similarly, ++ and −− each extend the range by an additional line, and so on. The + and − can also be used with search patterns, as shown in the next section.

The number 0 stands for the top of the file (imaginary line 0). 0 is equivalent to 1−, and both allow you to move or copy lines to the very start of a file, before the first line of existing text. For example:

> :−,+t0   Copy three lines (the line above the cursor through the line below the cursor) and put them at the top of the file.

Search Patterns

Another way that *ex* can address lines is by using search patterns. For example:

> :/pattern/d   Delete the next line containing *pattern*.

> :/pattern/+d   Delete the line *below* the next line containing *pattern*. (You could also use +1 instead of + alone.)

> :/pattern1/,/pattern2/d
> Delete from the first line containing *pattern1* through the first line containing *pattern2*.

> :.,/pattern/m23
> Take text from current line (.) through the first line containing *pattern* and put after line 23.

Note that patterns are delimited by a slash both *before* and *after*.

---

*In a relative address, you shouldn't separate the plus or minus symbol from the number that follows it. For example, +10 means "10 lines following," but + 10 means "11 lines following (1 + 10)," which is probably not what you mean.

If you make deletions by pattern with *vi* and *ex*, there is a difference in the way the two editors operate. Suppose you have in your file *practice* the lines:

```
With a screen editor you can scroll the
page, move the cursor, delete lines, insert
characters and more, while seeing results
of your edits as you make them.
```

Keystrokes   **Result**

`d/while`
```
With a screen editor you can scroll the
page, move the cursor, while seeing results
of your edits as you make them.
```

The *vi* delete to *pattern* command deletes from the cursor up to the word *while* but leaves the remainder of both lines.

`:.,/while/d`
```
With a screen editor you can scroll the
of your edits as you make them.
```

The *ex* command deletes the entire range of addressed lines; in this case both the current line and the line containing the pattern. All lines are deleted in their entirety.

Redefining the Current Line Position

Sometimes, using a relative line address in a command can give you unexpected results. For example, suppose the cursor is on line 1, and you want to print line 100 plus the five lines below it. If you type:

`:100,+5 p`

you'll get an error message saying, "First address exceeds second." The reason the command fails is that the second address is calculated relative to the current cursor position (line 1), so your command is really saying this:

`:100,6 p`

What you need is some way to tell the command to think of line 100 as the "current line," even though the cursor is on line 1.

ex provides such a way. When you use a semicolon instead of a comma, the first line address is recalculated as the current line. For example, the command:

```
:100;+5 p
```

prints the desired lines. The +5 is now calculated relative to line 100. A semicolon is useful with search patterns as well as absolute addresses. For example, to print the next line containing *pattern*, plus the 10 lines that follow it, enter the command:

```
:/pattern/;+10 p
```

Global Searches

You already know how to use / (slash) in *vi* to search for patterns of characters in your files. *ex* has a global command, g, that lets you search for a pattern and display all lines containing the pattern when it finds them. The command :g! does the opposite of :g. Use :g! (or its synonym :v) to search for all lines that do *not* contain *pattern*.

You can use the global command on all lines in the file, or you can use line addresses to limit a global search to specified lines or to a range of lines.

:g/*pattern*	Finds (moves to) the last occurrence of *pattern* in the file.
:g/*pattern*/p	Finds and displays all lines in the file containing *pattern*.
:g!/*pattern*/nu	Finds and displays all lines in the file that don't contain *pattern*; also displays line number for each line found.
:60,124g/*pattern*/p	Finds and displays any lines between lines 60 and 124 containing *pattern*.

As you might expect, g can also be used for global replacements. We'll talk about that in Chapter 6, *Global Replacement*.

Combining ex Commands

You don't always need to type a colon to begin a new *ex* command. In *ex*, the vertical bar (|) is a command separator, allowing you to combine multiple commands from the same *ex* prompt (in much the same way that a semicolon separates multiple commands at the UNIX shell prompt). When you use the | , keep track of the line addresses you specify. If one command affects the order of lines in the file, the next command does its work using the new line positions. For example:

:1,3d | s/thier/their/
    Delete lines 1 through 3 (leaving you now on the top line of the file); then make a substitution on the current line (which was line 4 before you invoked the *ex* prompt).

:1,5 m 10 | g/*pattern*/nu
    Move lines 1 through 5 after line 10, and then display all lines (with numbers) containing *pattern*.

Note the use of spaces to make the commands easier to see.

Saving and Exiting Files

You have learned the *vi* command Z Z to quit and write (save) your file. But you will usually want to exit a file using *ex* commands, because these commands give you greater control. We've already mentioned some of these commands in passing. Now let's take a more formal look.

:w   Writes (saves) the buffer to the file but does not exit. You can (and should) use :w throughout your editing session to protect your edits against system failure or a major editing error.

:q   Quits the file (and returns to the UNIX prompt).

:wq Both writes and quits the file.

:x   Both writes and quits (exits) the file. It's the same as :wq.

vi protects existing files and your edits in the buffer. For example, if you want to write your buffer to an existing file, *vi* gives you a warning. Likewise, if you have invoked *vi* on a file, made edits, and want to quit *without* saving the edits, *vi* gives you an error message such as:

```
No write since last change.
```

These warnings can prevent costly mistakes, but sometimes you want to proceed with the command anyway. An exclamation point (!) after your command overrides the warning:

```
:w!
:q!
```

w ! can also be used to save edits in a file that was opened in read-only mode with vi -R or view.

:q! is an essential editing command that allows you to quit without affecting the original file, regardless of any changes you made in this session. The contents of the buffer are discarded.

Renaming the Buffer

You can also use :w to save the entire buffer (the copy of the file you are editing) under a new filename.

Suppose you have a file *practice*, containing 600 lines. You open the file and make extensive edits. You want to quit but save *both* the old version of *practice* and your new edits for comparison. To save the edited buffer in a file called *practice.new*, give the command:

```
:w practice.new
```

Your old version, in the file *practice*, remains unchanged (provided that you didn't previously use :w). You can now quit the old version by typing :q.

Saving Part of a File

While editing, you will sometimes want to save just part of your file as a separate, new file. For example, you might have entered formatting codes and text that you want to use as a header for several files.

You can combine *ex* line addressing with the write command, w, to save part of a file. For example, if you are in the file *practice* and want to save part of practice as the file *newfile*, you could enter:

`:230,$w newfile`   Saves from line 230 to end of file in *newfile*.

`:.,600w newfile`   Saves from the current line to line 600 in *newfile*.

Appending to a Saved File

You can use the UNIX redirect and append operator (>>) with w to append all or part of the contents of the buffer to an existing file. For example, if you entered:

`:1,10w newfile`

then:

`:340,$w >>newfile`

newfile would contain lines 1-10 and from line 340 to the end of the buffer.

Copying a File into Another File

Sometimes you want to copy text or data already entered on the system into the file you are editing. In *vi* you can read in the contents of another file with the *ex* command:

`:read filename`

or its abbreviation:

`:r filename`

This command inserts the contents of *filename* starting on the line after the cursor position in the file. If you want to specify a line other than the one the cursor's on, simply type the line number (or other line address) you want before the read or r command.

Let's suppose you are editing the file *practice* and want to read in a file called *data* from another directory called */usr/tim*. Position the cursor one line above the line where you want the new data inserted, and enter:

```
:r /usr/tim/data
```

The entire contents of */usr/tim/data* are read into *practice*, beginning below the line with the cursor.

To read in the same file and place it after line 185, you would enter:

```
:185r /usr/tim/data
```

Here are other ways to read in a file:

`:$r /usr/tim/data`	Place the read-in file at the end of the current file.
`:0r /usr/tim/data`	Place the read-in file at the very beginning of the current file.
`:/pattern/r /usr/tim/data`	
	Place the read-in file in the current file, after the line containing *pattern*.

Editing Multiple Files

ex commands enable you to switch between multiple files. The advantage to editing multiple files is speed. When you are sharing the system with other users, it takes time to exit and reenter *vi* for each file you want to edit. Staying in the same editing session and traveling between files is not only faster for access, but you also save abbreviations and command sequences that you have defined (see Chapter 7, *Advanced Editing*), and you keep yank buffers so that you can copy text from one file to another.

Invoking vi on Multiple Files

When you first invoke *vi*, you can name more than one file to edit, and then use *ex* commands to travel between the files.

```
$ vi file1 file2
```

invokes *file1* first. After you have finished editing the first file, the *ex* command : w writes (saves) *file1* and : n calls in the next file (*file2*).

Suppose you want to edit two files, *practice* and *note*.

Keystrokes   **Result**

vi practice note

> With a screen editor you can scroll the
> the page, move the cursor, delete lines,
> insert characters, and more, while seeing

Open the two files *practice* and *note*. The first-named file, *practice*,
appears on your screen. Perform any edits.

:w

> "practice" 6 lines 328 characters

Save the edited file *practice* with the *ex* command w. Press RETURN.

:n

> Dear Mr.
> Henshaw:
> Thank you for the prompt . . .

Call in the next file, *note*, with the *ex* command n. Press RETURN.
Perform any edits.

:x

> "note" 23 lines 1343 characters

Save the second file, *note*, and quit the editing session.

Calling In New Files

You don't have to call in multiple files at the beginning of your editing
session. You can switch to another file at any time with the *ex*
command :e. If you want to edit another file within *vi*, you first need
to save your current file (:w), then give the command:

> :e *filename*

Suppose you are editing the file *practice* and want to edit the file *letter*,
then return to *practice*.

Keystrokes   **Result**

: w

"practice" 6 lines 328 characters

Save *practice* with w and press RETURN. *practice* is saved and remains on the screen. You can now switch to another file, because your edits are saved.

:e letter

"letter" 23 lines 1344 characters

Call in the file *letter* with e and press RETURN. Perform any edits.

vi "remembers" two filenames at a time as the current and alternate filenames. These can be referred to by the symbols % (current filename) and # (alternate filename). # is particularly useful with :e, since it allows you to switch easily back and forth between two files. In the example given just above, you could return to the first file, *practice*, by typing the command :e#. You could also read the file *practice* into the current file by typing :r#.

If you have not first saved the current file, *vi* will not allow you to switch files with :e or :n unless you tell it imperatively to do so by adding an exclamation point after the command.

For example, if after making some edits to *letter*, you wanted to discard the edits and return to *practice*, you could type :e!#.

The command:

　　:e!

is also useful. It discards your edits and returns to the last saved version of the current file.

In contrast to the # symbol, % is useful mainly when writing out the contents of the current buffer to a new file. For example, a few pages earlier, in the section "Renaming the Buffer," we showed how to save a second version of the file *practice* with the command:

　　:w practice.new

Since % stands for the current filename, the previous line could also have been typed:

```
:w %.new
```

Edits Between Files

When you give a yank buffer a one-letter name, you have a convenient way to move text from one file to another. Named buffers are not cleared when a new file is loaded into the *vi* buffer with the :e command. Thus, by yanking or deleting text from one file (into multiple named buffers if necessary), calling in a new file with :e, and putting the named buffer into the new file, you can transfer material between files.

The following example illustrates how to transfer text from one file to another.

Keystrokes   **Result**

`"f4yy`

```
With a screen editor you can scroll
the page, move the cursor, delete lines,
insert characters, and more, while seeing
the results of the edits as you make them
```

Yank four lines into buffer f.

`:w`

```
"practice" 6 lines 238 characters
```

Save the file.

`:e letter`

```
Dear Mr.
Henshaw:
I thought that you would
be interested to know that:
Yours truly,
```

Enter the file *letter* with :e. Move cursor to where the copied text will be placed.

"fp

```
Dear Mr.
Henshaw:
I thought that you would
be interested to know that:
With a screen editor you can scroll
the page, move the cursor, delete lines,
insert characters, and more, while seeing
the results of the edits as you make them
Yours truly,
```

Place yanked text from named buffer f below the cursor.

Another way to move text from one file to another is to use the *ex* commands :ya (yank) and :pu (put). These commands work the same way as the equivalent *vi* commands y and p, but they are used with *ex*'s line addressing capability and named buffers. For example:

    :160,224ya a

would yank (copy) lines 160 through 224 into buffer a. Next you would move with :e to the file where you want to put these lines. Place the cursor on the line where you want to put the yanked lines. Then type:

    :pu a

to put the contents of buffer a after the current line.

6

Global Replacement

Confirming Substitutions
Context-sensitive Replacement
Pattern-matching Rules
Pattern-matching Examples

Sometimes, halfway through a document or at the end of a draft, you may recognize inconsistencies in the way that you refer to certain things. Or, in a manual, some product whose name appears throughout your file is suddenly renamed (marketing!). Often enough it happens that you have to go back and change what you've already written, and you need to make the changes in several places.

The way to make these changes is with a powerful change command called global replacement. With one command you can automatically replace a word (or a string of characters) wherever it occurs in the file.

In a global replacement, the *ex* editor checks each line of a file for a given pattern of characters. On all lines where the pattern is found, *ex* replaces the pattern with a *new string* of characters. For right now, we'll treat the search pattern as if it were a simple string; later in the chapter we'll look at the powerful pattern-matching language known as *regular expressions*.

Global replacement really uses two _ex_ commands: : g (global) and : s (substitute). Since the syntax of global replacement commands can get fairly complex, let's look at it in stages.

The substitute command has the syntax:

```
:s/old/new/
```

This changes the first occurrence of the pattern _old_ to _new_ on the current line. The / (slash) is the delimiter between the various parts of the command. (The slash is optional when it is the last character on the line.) A substitute command with the syntax:

```
:s/old/new/g
```

changes _every_ occurrence of _old_ to _new_ on the current line, not just the first occurrence. The : s command allows options following the substitution string. The g option in the syntax above stands for _global_. (The g option affects each pattern on a line; don't confuse it with the : g command, which affects each line of a file.)

By prefixing the : s command with an address, you can extend its range to more than one line. For example:

```
:50,100s/old/new/g
```

will change every occurrence of _old_ to _new_ from line 50 to line 100.

The following command will change every occurrence of _old_ to _new_ within the entire file:

```
:1,$s/old/new/g
```

You can also use % instead of 1, $ to specify every line in a file. Thus the last command could also be given like this:

```
:%s/old/new/g
```

Global replacement is much faster than finding each instance of a string and replacing it individually. Because the command can be used to make many different kinds of changes, and because it is so powerful, we are first going to illustrate simple replacements and then build to complex, context-sensitive replacements.

Confirming Substitutions

It makes sense to be overly careful when using a search and replace command. It sometimes happens that what you get is not what you expect. You can undo any search and replacement command by entering u, provided that the command was the most recent edit you made. But you don't always catch undesired changes until it is too late to undo them. Another way to protect your edited file is to save the file with : w before performing a global replacement. Then at least you can quit the file without saving your edits and go back to where you were before the change was made. You can also read the previous version of the buffer back in with : e !.

It's wise to be cautious and know exactly what is going to be changed in your file. If you'd like to see what the search turns up and confirm each replacement before it is made, add the c option (for confirm) at the end of the substitute command:

```
:1,30s/his/the/gc
```

It will display the entire line where the string has been located and the string will be marked by a series of carets (^^^^).

```
copyists at his school
               ^ ^ ^
               _
```

If you want to make the replacement, you must enter y (for yes) and press RETURN. If you don't want to make a change, simply press RETURN.

```
this can be used for invitations, signs, and menus.
     ^ ^ ^
     _
```

The combination of the *vi* commands n (repeat last search) and dot (.) (repeat last command) is also an extraordinarily useful and quick way to page through a file and make repetitive changes that you may not want to make globally. So, for example, if your editor has told you that you're using *which* when you should be using *that*, you can spot-check every occurrence of *which*, changing only those that are incorrect:

which	Search for *which*.
cwthat ESC	Change to *that*.
n	Repeat search.
.	Repeat change (if appropriate).

.

.

.

Context-sensitive Replacement

The simplest global replacements substitute one word (or a phrase) for another. If you have typed a file with several misspellings (*editer* for *editor*), you can do the global replacement:

    :%s/editer/editor/g

This substitutes *editor* for every occurrence of *editer* throughout the file.

There is a second, slightly more complex syntax for global replacement. This syntax lets you search for a pattern, and then, once you find the line with the pattern, make a substitution on a string different from the pattern. You can think of this as context-sensitive replacement.

The syntax is as follows:

    :g/pattern/s/old/new/g

The first g tells the command to operate on all lines of a file. *pattern* identifies the lines on which a substitution is to take place. On those lines containing *pattern*, *ex* is to substitute (s) for *old* the characters in *new*. The last g indicates that the substitution is to occur globally *on that line*.

For example, in this handbook, the macro .BX places a box around ESC to show the ESCAPE key. You want ESC to be all in caps, but you don't want to change any instances of *Escape* that might be in the text. To change instances of *Esc* to *ESC* only when *Esc* is on a line starting with the .BX macro, you could enter:

```
:g/BX/s/Esc/ESC/g
```

If the pattern being used to find the line is the same as the one you want to change, you don't have to repeat it. The command:

```
:g/string/s//new/g
```

would search for lines containing *string* and substitute for that same *string*.

Note that:

```
:g/editer/s//editor/g
```

has the same effect as:

```
:%s/editer/editor/g
```

You can save some typing by using the second form. It is also possible to combine the :g command with :d, :mo, :co and other *ex* commands besides :s. As we'll show, you can thus make global deletions, moves and copies.

Pattern-matching Rules

In making global replacements, UNIX editors such as *vi* allow you to search not just for fixed strings of characters, but also for variable patterns of words, referred to as *regular expressions*.

When you specify a literal string of characters, the search might turn up other occurrences that you didn't want to match. The problem with searching for words in a file is that a word can be used in different ways. Regular expressions help you conduct a search for words in context. Note that regular expressions can be used with the *vi* search commands / and ? as well as in the *ex* :g and :s commands. For the most part, the same regular expressions work with other UNIX programs such as grep, sed, and awk.

Regular expressions are made up by combining normal characters with a number of special characters called *metacharacters*. The metacharacters and their uses are listed below.

Metacharacters Used in Search Patterns

.   Matches any *single* character except a newline (carriage return). Remember that spaces are treated as characters. For example, p.p matches character strings such as *pep, pip, pcp*.

*   Matches any number (or none) of the single character that immediately precedes it. For example, bugs* will match *bugs* (one *s*) or *bug* (no *s*'s).

       The character preceding the * can be one that is specified by a regular expression. For example, since . (dot) means any character, .* means "match any number of any character."

       Here's a specific example of this. The command :s/End.*/End/ removes all characters after *End* (it replaces the remainder of the line with nothing).

^   Requires that the following regular expression be found at the beginning of the line; for example, ^Part matches *Part* when it occurs at the beginning of a line, and ^ . . . matches the first three characters of a line.

$ Requires that the preceding regular expression be found at the end of the line; for example, here:$.

\   Treats the following special character as an ordinary character. For example, \. matches an actual period instead of "any single character," and * matches an actual asterisk instead of "any number of a character." The \ (backslash) prevents the interpretation of a special character. This prevention is called "escaping the character."

[   ]   Matches any *one* of the characters enclosed between the brackets. For example, [AB] matches either *A* or *B*, and p[aeiou]t matches *pat, pet, pit, pot,* or *put*. A range of consecutive characters can be specified by separating the first and last characters in the range with a hyphen. For example, [A-Z] will match any uppercase letter from *A* to *Z*, and [0-9] will match any digit from *0* to *9*.

You can include more than one range inside brackets, and you can specify a mix of ranges and separate characters. For example, [:;A-Za-z()] will match four different punctuation marks, plus all letters.

Most metacharacters lose their special meaning inside brackets, so you don't need to escape them if you want to use them as ordinary characters. Within brackets, the three metacharacters you still need to escape are \ -]. (The hyphen (-) acquires meaning as a range specifier; to use an actual hyphen, you can also place it as the the first character inside the brackets.)

A caret (^) has special meaning only when it is the first character inside the brackets, but in this case the meaning differs from that of the normal ^ metacharacter. As the first character within brackets, a ^ reverses their sense: the brackets will match any one character *not* in the list. For example, [^a-z] matches any character that is not a lowercase letter.

\(\)   Saves the pattern enclosed between \ (and \ ) into a special holding space or "hold buffer." Up to nine patterns can be saved in this way on a single line. For example, the pattern:

```
\(That\) or \(this\)
```

saves *That* in hold buffer number 1 and saves *this* in hold buffer number 2. The patterns held can be "replayed" in substitutions by the sequences \ 1 to \ 9. For example, to rephrase *That or this* to read *this or That*, you could enter:

```
:%s/\(That\) or \(this\)/\2 or \1/
```

\<   \>   Matches characters at the beginning (\ <) or at the end (\ >) of a word. The end or beginning of a word is determined either by a punctuation mark or by a space. For example, the expression \ <ac will match only words that begin with *ac*, such as *action*. The expression ac \ > will match only words that end with *ac*, such as *maniac*. Neither expression will match *react*.

~ Matches whatever regular expression was used in the *last* search. For example, if you searched for *The*, you could search for *Then* with /~n. Note that you can use this pattern only in a regular search (with /). It won't work as the pattern in a substitute command. It does, however, have a similar meaning in the replacement portion of a substitute command.

Metacharacters Used in Replacement Strings

When you make global replacements, the regular expressions above carry their special meaning only within the search portion (the first part) of the command. For example, when you type this:

```
:%s/1\.  Start/2.  Next, start with $100/
```

note that the replacement string understands the characters . and $, without your having to escape them. By the same token, let's say you enter:

```
:%s/[ABC]/[abc]/g
```

If you're hoping to replace *A* with *a*, *B* with *b*, and *C* with *c*, you're in for a surprise. Since brackets behave like ordinary characters in a replacement string, this command will change every occurrence of *A*, *B*, or *C* to the five-character string *[abc]*.

To solve problems like this, you need a way to specify variable replacement strings. Fortunately, there are additional regular expressions that have special meaning in a *replacement* string.

\n   Matches the *n*th pattern previously saved by \(and \), where *n* is a number from 0 to 9, and previously saved patterns are counted from the left on the line. See the explanation for \(and \) in the previous section.

\   Treats the following special character as an ordinary character. Backslashes are metacharacters in replacement strings as well as in search patterns. To specify a real backslash, type two in a row (\\).

&   Prints the entire search pattern when used in a replacement string. This is useful when you want to avoid retyping text:

```
:%s/Yazstremski/&, Carl/
```

The replacement will say *Yazstremski, Carl.* The & can also replace a variable pattern (as specified by a regular expression). For example, to add *(check this)* to the end of lines 1 through 10, type:

```
:1,10s/.*/& (check this)/
```

The search pattern matches the whole line, and the & "replays" the line, followed by your text.

~   Has a similar meaning as when it is used in a search pattern; the string found is replaced with the replacement text specified in the last substitute command. This is useful for repeating an edit. For example, you could say `:s/thier/their/` on one line and repeat the change on another with `:s/thier/~/`. The search pattern doesn't need to be the same, though. For example, you could say `:s/his/their/` on one line and repeat the replacement on another with `:s/her/~/`.

\u or \l   Causes the next character in the replacement string to be changed to uppercase or lowercase, respectively. For example, to change *yes, doctor* into *Yes, Doctor*, you could say:

```
:%s/yes, doctor/\uyes, \udoctor/
```

This is a pointless example, though, since it's easier just to type the replacement string with initial caps in the first place. As with any regular expression, \u and \l are most useful with a variable string. Take, for example, the command we used earlier:

```
:%s/\(That\) or \(this\)/\2 or \1/
```

The result is *this or That,* but we need to adjust the cases. We'll use \u to uppercase the first letter in *this* (currently saved in hold buffer 2); we'll use \l to lowercase the first letter in *That* (currently saved in hold buffer 1):

```
:s/\(That\) or \(this\)/\u\2 or \l\1/
```

The result is *This or that.* (Don't confuse the number one with the lowercase l; the one comes after.)

\U or \L   Similar to \u or \l, but all following characters are converted to uppercase or lowercase until the end of the replacement string or until \e or \E is reached. If there is no \e or \E, all characters of the replacement text are affected by the \U or \L. For example, to uppercase *Fortran*, you could say:

```
:%s/Fortran/\UFortran/
```

or, using the & character to repeat the search string:

```
:%s/Fortran/\U&/
```

All pattern searches are case-sensitive. That is, a search for *the* will not find *The*. You can get around this by specifying both uppercase and lowercase in the pattern:

```
/[Tt]he
```

You can also instruct *vi* to ignore case by typing :set ic. See Chapter 7, *Advanced Editing*, for additional details.

Pattern-matching Examples

Unless you are already familiar with regular expressions, the discussion of special characters above probably looks forbiddingly complex. A few more examples should make things clearer. In the examples that follow, a square (□) is used to mark a blank space; it is not a special character.

Let's work through how you might use some special characters in a replacement. Suppose that you have a long file and that you want to substitute the word *child* with the word *children* throughout that file. You first save the edited buffer with :w, then try the global replacement:

```
:%s/child/children/g
```

When you continue editing, you notice occurrences of words such as *childrenish*. You have unintentionally matched the word *childish*. Returning to the last saved buffer with :e!, you now try:

```
:%s/child□/children□/g
```

(Note that there is a space after *child*.) But this command misses the occurrences *child.*, *child,*, *child:* and so on. After some thought, you remember that brackets allow you to specify one character from among a list, so you come upon the solution:

```
:%s/child[□,.;:!?]/children[□,.;:!?]/g
```

This searches for *child* followed by either a space (indicated by □) or any one of the punctuation characters `,.;:!?`. You expect to replace this with *children* followed by the corresponding space or punctuation mark, but you've ended up with a bunch of punctuation marks after every occurrence of *children*. You need to save the space and punctuation marks inside a \ (and \). Then you can "replay" them with a \1. Here's the next attempt:

```
:%s/child\([□,.;:!?]\)/children\1/g
```

When the search matches a character inside the \ (and \), the \1 on the right-hand side restores the same character. The syntax may seem awfully complicated, but this command sequence can save you a lot of work! *Any time you spend learning regular expression syntax will be repaid a thousandfold!*

The command is still not perfect, though. You've noticed that occurrences of *Fairchild* have been changed, so you need a way to match *child* when it isn't part of another word.

As it turns out, *vi* (but not all other programs that use regular expressions) has a special syntax for saying "only if the pattern is a complete word." The character sequence \< requires the pattern to match at the beginning of a word, whereas \> requires the pattern to match at the end of a word. Using both will restrict the match to a whole word. So, in the task given above, \<child\> will find all instances of the word *child*, whether followed by punctuation or spaces. Here's the substitution command you should use:

```
:%s/\<child\>/children/g
```

Search for General Class of Words

Suppose you have subroutine names beginning with the prefixes: *mgi*, *mgr* and *mga*.

```
mgibox routine,
mgrbox routine,
mgabox routine,
```

If you want to save the prefixes but want to change the name *box* to *square*, either of the following replacement commands will do the trick. The first example illustrates how \ (and \ ) can be used to save whatever pattern was actually matched. The second example shows how you can search for one pattern but change another.

```
:g/mg\([ira]\)box/s//mg\1square/g
```

```
mgisquare routine,
mgrsquare routine,
mgasquare routine,
```

The global replacement keeps track of whether an *i*, *r* or *a* is saved. In that way, *box* is changed to *square* only when *box* is part of the routine's name.

```
:g/mg[ira]box/s/box/square/g
```

```
mgisquare routine,
mgrsquare routine,
mgasquare routine,
```

Has the same effect as the previous command, but it is a little less safe since it could change other instances of *box* on the same line, not just those within the routine names.

Block Move by Patterns

You can also move blocks of text delimited by patterns. For example, assume you have a 150-page reference manual. All references pages are organized into three paragraphs with the same three headings: SYNTAX, DESCRIPTION, and PARAMETERS. A sample of one reference page follows:

```
.Rh 0 "Get status of named file" "STAT"
.Rh "SYNTAX"
.nf
integer*4 stat, retval
integer*4 status(11)
character*123 filename
...
retval = stat (filename, status)
.fi
.Rh "DESCRIPTION"
Writes the fields of a system data structure into the
status array.
These fields contain (among other
things) information about the file's location, access
privileges, owner, and time of last modification.
.Rh "PARAMETERS"
.IP "\fBfilename\fR" 15n
A character string variable or constant containing
the UNIX pathname for the file whose status you want
to retrieve.
You can give the ...
```

Suppose that it is decided to move DESCRIPTION above the SYNTAX paragraph. With pattern matching, you can move blocks of text on all 150 pages with one command!

```
:g /SYNTAX/,/DESCRIPTION/-1 mo /PARAMETERS/-1
```

This command operates on the block of text between the line containing the word *SYNTAX* and the line just before the word *DESCRIPTION* (/DESCRIPTION/-1). The block is moved (using mo) to the line just before *PARAMETERS* (/PARAMETERS/-1). Note that *ex* can place text only below the line specified. To tell *ex* to place text above a line, you first have to move up a line with -1, and then place your text below. In a case like this, one command saves literally hours of work. (This is a real-life example—we once used a pattern match like this to rearrange a reference manual containing hundreds of pages.)

Block definition by patterns can be used equally well with other *ex* commands. For example, if you wanted to delete all DESCRIPTION paragraphs in the reference chapter, you could enter:

```
:g/DESCRIPTION/,/PARAMETERS/-1d
```

This very powerful kind of change is implicit in *ex's* line addressing syntax, but it is not readily apparent even to experienced users. For this reason, whenever you are faced with a complex, repetitive editing task, take the time to analyze the problem and find out if you can apply pattern-matching tools to get the job done.

More Examples

Since the best way to learn pattern matching is by example, here is a list of pattern-matching examples, with explanations. Study the syntax carefully, so that you understand the principles at work. You should then be able to adapt these examples to your own situation.

1. Put *troff* italicization codes around the word *RETURN*:

   ```
   :%s/RETURN/\\fIRETURN\\fP/g
   ```

   Notice that two backslashes (\\) are needed in the replacement, because the backslash in the *troff* italicization code will be interpreted as a special character. (\fI alone would be interpreted as *fI*; you must type \\fI to get \fI.)

2. Modify a list of pathnames in a file:

   ```
   :%s/\usr\tim/\usr\linda/g
   ```

   A slash (used as a delimiter in the global replacement sequence) must be escaped with a backslash when it is part of the pattern or replacement; use \/ to get /. An alternate way to achieve this same effect is to use a different character as the pattern delimiter. For example, you could make the above replacement using colons as delimiters. Thus:

   ```
   :%s:/usr/tim:/usr/linda:g
   ```

3. Change all periods to semicolons in lines 1 to 10:

   ```
   :1,10s/\./;/g
   ```

   A dot has special meaning in regular expression syntax and must be escaped with a backslash (\.).

4. Change all occurrences of the word *help* (or *Help*) to *HELP*:

   ```
   :%s/[Hh]elp/HELP/g
   ```

   or:

```
:%s/[Hh]elp/\U&/g
```

The \U changes the pattern that follows to all uppercase. The pattern that follows is the repeated search pattern, which is either *help* or *Help*.

5. Replace *one or more* spaces with a single space:

```
:%s/□□*/□/g
```

Make sure you understand how the asterisk works as a special character. An asterisk following any character (or following any regular expression that matches a single character, such as . or [a-z]) matches *zero or more* instances of that character. Therefore, you must specify *two* spaces followed by an asterisk to match one or more spaces (one space, plus zero or more spaces).

6. Replace one or more spaces following a colon with two spaces:

```
:%s/:□□*/:□□/g
```

7. Replace one or more spaces following a period *or* a colon with two spaces:

```
:%s/\([:.]\)□□*/\1□□/g
```

Either of the two characters within brackets can be matched. This character is saved into a hold buffer, using \(and \), and restored on the right-hand side by the \1. Note that within brackets a special character such as a dot does not need to be escaped.

8. Standardize various uses of a word or heading:

```
:%s/^Note[□:s]*/Notes:□/g
```

The brackets enclose three characters: a space, a colon, and the letter *s*. Therefore, the pattern Note[□s:] will match *Note□*, *Notes* or *Note:*. An asterisk is added to the pattern so that it also matches *Note* (with zero spaces after it) and *Notes:* (the already correct spelling). Without the asterisk, *Note* would be missed entirely and *Notes:* would be incorrectly changed to *Notes:□:.*

9. Delete all blank lines:

```
:g/^$/d
```

What you are actually matching here is the beginning of the line (^) followed by the end of the line ($), with nothing in between.

10. Delete all blank lines, plus any lines that contain only white space:

    ```
    :g/^[□tab]*$/d
    ```

(In the line above, a tab is shown as *tab*.) A line may appear to be blank but may in fact contain spaces or tabs. The previous example will not delete such a line. This example, like the one above it, searches for the beginning and end of the line. But instead of having nothing in between, the pattern tries to find any number of spaces or tabs. If no spaces or tabs are matched, the line is blank. To delete lines that contain white space but that *aren't* blank, you would have to match lines with *at least* one space or tab:

    ```
    :g/^[□tab][□tab]*$/d
    ```

11. Delete all leading spaces on a line:

    ```
    :%s/^□□*\(.*\)/\1/
    ```

Use ^□□* to search for one or more spaces at the beginning of a line; then use \(.*\) to save the rest of the line into the first hold buffer. Restore the line without spaces, using \1.

12. Delete all spaces at the end of a line:

    ```
    :%s/\(.*\)□□*$/\1/
    ```

Use \(.*\) to save all the text on the line, but only up until one or more spaces at the end of the line. Restore the saved text without the spaces.

The substitutions in this example and the previous one will happen only once on any given line, so the g option doesn't need to follow the replacement string.

13. Insert a >□□ at the start of every line in a file:

    ```
    :%s/^/>□□/
    ```

What we're really doing here is "replacing" the start of the line with >□□. Of course, the start of the line (being a logical construct, not an actual character) isn't really replaced!

This command is useful when replying to mail or USENET news postings. Frequently, it is desirable to include part of the original message in your reply. By convention, the inclusion is distinguished from your reply by setting off the included text with a right angle bracket and a couple of spaces at the start of the line. This can be done easily as shown above. (Typically, only part of the original message will be included. Unneeded text can be deleted either before or after the above replacement.) Advanced mail systems do this automatically. However, if you're using a primitive mail program, you may need to do it manually.

14. Add a period to the end of the next six lines:

```
:.,+5s/$/./
```

The line address indicates the current line plus five lines. The $ indicates the end of line. As in the previous example, the $ is a logical construct. You aren't really replacing the end of the line.

15. Reverse the order of all hyphen-separated items in a list:

```
:%s/\(.*\)□-□\(.*\)/\2□-□\1/
```

Use \ (. * \ ) to save text on the line into the first hold buffer, but only until you find □-□. Then use \ (. * \ ) to save the rest of the line into the second hold buffer. Restore the saved portions of the line, reversing the order of the two hold buffers. The effect of this command on several items is shown below.

```
more - display files
```

becomes:

```
display files - more
```

and:

```
lp - print files
```

becomes:

```
print files - lp
```

16. Change every word in a file to uppercase:

```
:%s/.*/\U&/
```

or:

```
:%s/./\U&/g
```

The \U flag at the start of the replacement string tells *vi* to change the replacement to uppercase. The & character replays the search pattern as the replacement. These two commands are equivalent;

however, the first form is considerably faster, since it results in only one substitution per line (`.*` matches the entire line, once per line), whereas the second form results in repeated substitutions on each line (`.` matches only a single character, with the replacement repeated on account of the trailing g).

17. Reverse the order of lines in a file:*

    ```
    :g/.*/mo0
    ```

    The search pattern matches all lines (a line contains zero or more characters). Each line is moved, one by one, to the top of the file (that is, moved after imaginary line 0). As each matched line is placed at the top, it pushes the previously moved lines down, one by one, until the last line is on top.

    Since all lines have a beginning, the same result can be achieved more succinctly:

    ```
    :g/^/mo0
    ```

18. In a database, on all lines not marked *Paid in full*, append the phrase *Overdue*:

    ```
    :g!/Paid□in□full/s/$/Overdue/
    ```

    or the equivalent:

    ```
    :v/Paid□in□full/s/$/Overdue/
    ```

    To affect all lines *except* those matching your pattern, add a `!` to the g command, or simply use the v command.

19. For any line that doesn't begin with a number, move the line to the end of the file:

    ```
    :g!/^[1-9]/m$
    ```

    or:

    ```
    :g/^[^1-9]/m$
    ```

    As the first character within brackets, a caret negates the sense, so the two commands have the same effect. The first one says, "Don't match lines that begin with a number," and the second one says, "Match lines that don't begin with a number."

---

* From the article by Walter Zintz in *UNIX World*, May 1990.

20. Change manually numbered section heads (e.g., 1.1, 1.2, etc.) to a *troff* macro (e.g., *.Ah* for an A-level heading):

```
:%s/[1-9]\.[1-9]/.Ah/
```

The search string matches a digit other than zero, followed by a period, followed by another nonzero digit. Notice that the period doesn't need to be escaped in the replacement (though a \ would have no effect, either). The command above won't find chapter numbers containing two or more digits. To do so, modify the command like this:

```
:%s/[1-9][0-9]*\.[1-9]/.Ah/
```

Now it will match chapters 10 to 99 (digits 1 to 9, followed by a digit), 100 to 999 (digits 1 to 9, followed by two digits), etc. The command still finds chapters 1 to 9 (digits 1 to 9, followed by no digit).

21. Remove numbering from section headings in a document. You want to change the sample lines:

```
2.1 Introduction
10.3.8 New Functions
```

into the lines:

```
Introduction
New Functions
```

Here's the command to do this:

```
:%s/^[1-9][0-9]*\.[1-9][1-9.]*□\(.*\)/\1/
```

The search pattern resembles the one in the previous example, but now the numbers vary in length. At a minimum, the headings contain *number*, *period*, *number*, so you start with the search pattern from the previous example:

```
[1-9][0-9]*\.[1-9]
```

But in this example, the heading may continue with any number of digits or periods:

```
[1-9.]*
```

Finally, we save the rest of the line, leaving the space outside the hold buffer so that the restored text won't have a space before it.

22. Change the word *Fortran* to the phrase *FORTRAN (acronym of FORmula TRANslation)*:

```
:%s/\(For\)\(tran\)/\U\1\2\E□(acronym□of□\U\1\Emula□\U\2\Eslation)/g
```

First, since we notice that the words *FORmula* and *TRANslation* use portions of the original word, we decide to save the search pattern in two pieces: `\(For\)` and `\(tran\)`. The first time we restore it, we use both pieces together, converting all characters to uppercase: `\U\1\2`. Next, we undo the uppercase with `\E`; otherwise the remaining replacement text would all be uppercase. The replacement continues with actual typed words, then we restore the first hold buffer. This buffer still contains *For*, so again we convert to uppercase first: `\U\1`. Immediately after, we lowercase the rest of the word: `\Emula`. Finally, we restore the second hold buffer. This contains *tran*, so we precede the "replay" with uppercase, follow it with lowercase, and type out the rest of the word: `\U\2\Eslation)`.

A Final Look at Pattern Matching

We conclude this chapter by presenting sample tasks that involve complex pattern-matching concepts. Rather than solve the problems right away, we'll work toward the solutions step by step.

Deleting an Unknown Block of Text

Suppose you have a few lines with this general form:

```
    the best of times; the worst of times:  moving
    The coolest of times; the worst of times:  moving
```

The lines that you're concerned with always end with *moving*, but you never know what the first two words might be. You want to change any line that ends with *moving* to read:

```
    The greatest of times; the worst of times:  moving
```

Since the changes must occur on certain lines, you need to specify a context-sensitive global replacement. Using `:g/moving$/` will match lines that end with *moving*. Next, you realize that your search pattern could be any number of any character, so the metacharacters

.* come to mind. But these will match the whole line unless you somehow restrict the match. Here's your first attempt:

```
:g/moving$/s/.*of/The□greatest□of/
```

This search string, you decide, will match from the beginning of the line to the first *of*. Since you needed to specify the word *of* to restrict the search, you simply repeat it in the replacement. Here's the resulting line:

```
The greatest of times:   moving
```

Something went wrong. The replacement gobbled the line up to the second *of* instead of the first. Here's why. When given a choice, the action of "match any number of any character" will match as much text as possible. In this case, since the word *of* appears twice, your search string finds:

```
the best of times; the worst of
```

rather than:

```
the best of
```

Your search pattern needs to be more restrictive:

```
:g/moving$/s/.*of times;/The greatest of times;/
```

Now the .* will match all characters up to the instance of the phrase *of times;*. Since there's only one instance, it has to be the first.

There are cases, though, when it is inconvenient, or even incorrect, to use the .* metacharacters. For example, you might find yourself typing many words to restrict your search pattern, or you might be unable to restrict the pattern by specific words (if the text in the lines varies widely). The next section presents such a case.

Switching Items in a Database

Suppose you want to switch the order of all last names and first names in a database. The lines look like this:

```
Name: Feld, Ray; Areas: PC, UNIX; Phone: 123-4567
Name: Joy, Susan S.; Areas: Graphics; Phone: 999-3333
```

The name of each field ends with a colon, and each field is separated by a semicolon. Using the top line as an example, you want to change *Feld, Ray* to *Ray Feld*. We'll present some commands that look promising but don't work. After each command, we show you the line the way it looked before the change and after the change.

```
:%s/: \(.*\), \(.*\);/: \2 \1;/
```

Name: **Feld, Ray;** **Areas: PC,** *UNIX;* Phone: 123-4567   *Before*
Name: *UNIX* **Feld, Ray;** **Areas: PC;** Phone: 123-4567   *After*

We've highlighted the contents of the first hold buffer in **bold** and the contents of the second hold buffer in *italic*. Note that the first hold buffer contains more than you want. Since it was not sufficiently restricted by the pattern that follows it, the hold buffer was able to save up to the second comma. Now you try to restrict the contents of the first hold buffer:

```
:%s/: \(....\), \(.*\);/: \2 \1;/
```

Name: **Feld,** *Ray; Areas: PC, UNIX;* Phone: 123-4567   *Before*
Name: *Ray; Areas: PC, UNIX* **Feld;** Phone: 123-4567   *After*

Here you've managed to save the last name in the first hold buffer, but now the second hold buffer will save anything up to the last semicolon on the line. Now you restrict the second hold buffer, too:

```
:%s/: \(....\), \(...\);/: \2 \1;/
```

Name: **Feld,** *Ray;* Areas: PC, UNIX; Phone: 123-4567   *Before*
Name: *Ray* **Feld;** Areas: PC, UNIX; Phone: 123-4567   *After*

This gives you what you want, but only in the specific case of a four-letter last name and a three-letter first name. (The previous attempt included the same mistake.) Why not just return to the first attempt, but this time be more selective about the end of the search pattern?

```
:%s/: \(.*\), \(.*\); Area/: \2 \1;/
```

Name: **Feld,** *Ray;* Areas: PC, UNIX; Phone: 123-4567   *Before*
Name: *Ray* **Feld;** Areas: PC, UNIX; Phone: 123-4567   *After*

This works, but we'll continue the discussion by introducing an additional concern. Suppose that the *Area* field isn't always present or isn't always the second field. The above command won't work on such lines.

We introduce this problem to make a point. Whenever you rethink a pattern match, it's usually better to work toward refining the variables (the metacharacters), rather than using specific text to restrict patttterns.

The more variables you use in your patterns, the more powerful your commands will be.

In the current example, think again about the patterns you want to switch. Each word starts with an uppercase letter and is followed by any number of lowercase letters, so you can match the names like this:

```
[A-Z][a-z]*
```

Ok, but a last name might also have more than one uppercase letter (*McFly*, for example), so you'd want to search for this possibility in the second and succeeding letters:

```
[A-Z][A-Za-z]*
```

It doesn't hurt to use this for the first name, too (you never know when *McGeorge Bundy* will turn up). Your command now becomes:

```
:%s/: \([A-Z][A-Za-z]*\), \([A-Z][A-Za-z]*\);/: \2 \1;/
```

Quite forbidding, isn't it? It still doesn't cover the case of a name like *Joy, Susan S*. Since the first-name field might include a middle initial, you need to add a space and a period within the second pair of brackets. But enough is enough. Sometimes, specifying exactly what you want is more difficult than specifying what you *don't* want. In your sample database, the last names end with a comma, so a last-name field can be thought of as a string of characters that are *not* commas:

```
[^,]*
```

This pattern matches characters up until the first comma. Similarly, the first-name field is a string of characters that are *not* semicolons:

```
[^;]*
```

Putting these more efficient patterns back into your previous command, you get this:

```
:%s/: \([^,]*\), \([^;]*\);/: \2 \1;/
```

The same command could also be entered as a context-sensitive replacement. If all lines begin with *Name*, you can say:

```
:g/^Name/: \([^,]*\), \([^;]*\);/: \2 \1;/
```

You can also add an asterisk after the first space, in order to match a colon that has extra spaces (or no spaces) after it:

```
:g/^Name/: *\([^,]*\), \([^;]*\);/: \2 \1;/
```

Using :g to Repeat a Command

As we've usually seen the `:g` command used, it selects lines that are typically then edited by subsequent commands on the same line—for example, we select lines with `g`, and then make substitutions on them, or select them and delete them:

```
:g/mg[ira]box/s/box/square/g
:g/^$/d
```

However, in his two-part tutorial in *UNIX World**, Walter Zintz makes an interesting point about the `g` command. This command selects lines—but the associated editing commands need not actually affect the lines that are selected.

Instead, he demonstrates a technique by which you can repeat *ex* commands some arbitrary number of times. For example, suppose you want to place ten copies of lines 12 through 17 of your file at the end of your current file. You could type:

```
:1,10g/^/ 12,17t$
```

This is a very unexpected use of `g`, but it works! The `g` command selects line 1, executes the specified `t` command, then goes on to line 2, to execute the next copy command. When line 10 is reached, *ex* will have made ten copies.

Collecting Lines

Here's another advanced `g` example, again building on suggestions provided in Zintz's article. Suppose you're editing a document that consists of several parts. Part 2 of this file is shown below, using ellipses to show omitted text and displaying line numbers for reference.

---

*Part 1, "vi Tips for Power Users," appears in the April 1990 issue of *UNIX World*. Part 2, "Using *vi* to Automate Complex Edits," appears in the May 1990 issue. The examples presented are from Part 2.

```
301  Part 2
302  Capability Reference
303  .LP
304  Chapter 7
305  Introduction to the Capabilities
306  This and the next three chapters ...

400  ... and a complete index at the end.
401  .LP
402  Chapter 8
403  Screen Dimensions
404  Before you can do anything useful
405  on the screen, you need to know ...

555  .LP
556  Chapter 9
557  Editing the Screen
558  This chapter discusses ...

821  .LP
822  Part 3:
823  Advanced Features
824  .LP
825  Chapter 10 ...
```

The chapter numbers appear on one line, their titles appear on the line below, and the chapter text (highlighted for emphasis) begins on the line below that. The first thing you'd like to do is copy the beginning line of each chapter, sending it to an already existing file called *begin*.

Here's the command that does this:

```
:g /^Chapter/ .+2w >> begin
```

You must be at the top of your file before issuing this command. First you search for *Chapter* at the start of a line, but then you want to run the command on the beginning line of each chapter—the second line below *Chapter*. Because a line beginning with *Chapter* is now selected as the current line, the line address .+2 will indicate the second line below it. The equivalent line addresses +2 or ++ work as well. You want to write these lines to an existing file named *begin*, so you issue the w command with the append operator >>.

Suppose you want to send the beginnings of chapters that are only within Part 2. You need to restrict the lines selected by g, so you change your command to this:

```
:/^Part 2/,/^Part 3/g /^Chapter/ .+2w >> begin
```

Here, the g command selects the lines that begin with *Chapter*, but it searches only that portion of the file from a line starting with *Part 2* through a line starting with *Part 3*. If you issue the above command, the last lines of the file *begin* will read as follows:

```
This and the next three chapters ...
Before you can do anything useful
This chapter discusses ...
```

These are the lines that begin Chapters 7, 8, and 9.

In addition to the lines you've just sent, you'd like to copy chapter titles to the end of the document, in preparation for making a table of contents. You can use the vertical bar to tack a second command after your first command, like so:

```
:/^Part 2/,/^Part 3/g /^Chapter/ .+2w >> begin | +t$
```

Remember that with any subsequent command, line addresses are relative to the previous command. The first command has marked lines (within Part 2) that start with *Chapter*, and the chapter titles appear on a line below such lines. Therefore, to access chapter titles in the second command, the line address is + (or the equivalents +1 or .+1). Then use t$ to copy the chapter titles to the end of the file.

As these examples illustrate, thought and experimentation may lead you to some unusual editing solutions. Don't be afraid to try things! Just be sure to back up your file first.

7

Advanced Editing

Customizing vi
Executing UNIX Commands
Saving Commands
Using ex Scripts
Editing Program Source Code

This chapter introduces you to some of the more advanced capabilities of the *vi* and *ex* editors. You should be reasonably familiar with the material presented in the earlier chapters of this book before you start working with the concepts presented in this chapter.

This chapter is divided into five parts. The first part discusses a number of ways to set options that allow you to customize your editing environment. You'll learn how to use the set command and how to create a number of different editing environments using *.exrc* files.

The second part discusses how you can execute UNIX commands from within *vi*, and how you can use *vi* to filter text through UNIX commands.

The third part discusses various ways to save long sequences of commands by reducing them to abbreviations, or even to commands that use only one keystroke (this is called *mapping* keys). It also includes a section on @-functions, which allow you to store command sequences in a buffer.

The fourth part discusses the use of *ex* scripts from the UNIX command line or from within shell scripts. Scripting provides a powerful way to make repetitive edits.

The fifth part discusses some features of *vi* that are especially useful to programmers. *vi* has options that control line indentation and an option to display invisible characters (specifically tabs and newlines). There are search commands that are useful with program code blocks or with C functions.

Customizing vi

You have seen that *vi* operates differently on various terminals. (For instance, on "dumb" terminals, *vi* inserts @ symbols in place of deleted lines; on intelligent terminals, *vi* redraws the screen with each edit.) *vi* gets operating instructions about your terminal type from a file called */etc/termcap*. (In System V, *termcap* has been replaced with an alternate terminal database called *terminfo*.)

There are also a number of options that you can set from within *vi* that affect how it operates. For example, you can set a right margin that will cause *vi* to wrap lines automatically, so you don't need to insert carriage returns.

You can change options from within *vi* by using the *ex* command : set. In addition, whenever *vi* is started up, it reads a file in your home directory called *.exrc* for further operating instructions. By placing : set commands in this file, you can modify the way *vi* acts whenever you use it.

You can also set up *.exrc* files in local directories to initialize various options that you want to use in different environments. For example, you might define one set of options for editing English text, but another set for editing source programs. The *.exrc* file in your home directory will be executed first, then the one in your current directory.

Finally, any commands stored in the shell variable *EXINIT* will be executed by *vi* on startup. If there is a conflict between settings made in *.exrc* and *EXINIT*, those in *.exrc* take precedence.

The :set Command

There are two types of options that can be changed with the :set command: toggle options, which are either on or off, and options that take a numeric or string value (such as the location of a margin or the name of a file).

Toggle options may be on or off by default. To turn a toggle option on, the command is:

```
:set option
```

To turn a toggle option off, the command is:

```
:set nooption
```

For example, to specify that pattern searches should ignore case, type:

```
:set ic
```

If you want *vi* to return to being case-sensitive in searches, give the command:

```
:set noic
```

Some options have a value assigned to them. For example, the window option sets the number of lines shown in the screen's "window." You set values for these options with an equal sign (=):

```
:set window=20
```

During a *vi* session, you can check which options *vi* is using. The command:

```
:set all
```

displays the complete list of options, including options that you have set and defaults that *vi* has "chosen."

The display should look something like this:

```
noautoindent       nooptimize              tabstop=8
autoprint          open                    taglength=0
noautowrite        prompt                  term=wy50
nobeautify         noreadonly              noterse
directory=/tmp     redraw                  timeout
noedcompatible     remap                   ttytype=wy50
noerrorbells       report=5                warn
hardtabs=8         scroll=11               window=20
noignorecase       sections=AhBhChDh       wrapscan
nolisp             shell=/bin/csh          wrapmargin=10
nolist             noshowmatch             nowriteany
magic              noslowopen
mesg               paragraphs=IPLPPPQP LIpplpipbb
number             tags=tags /usr/lib/tags
```

You can find out the current value of any individual option by name, using the command:

```
:set option?
```

The command:

```
:set
```

shows options that you have specifically changed, or set, either in your *.exrc* file or during the current session. For example, the display might look like this:

```
number sect=AhBhChDh window=20 wrapmargin=10
```

The .exrc File

The *.exrc* file that controls your own *vi* environment is in your home directory (the directory you are in when you first log on). You can modify the *.exrc* file with the *vi* editor, just as you can any other text file.

If you don't yet have an *.exrc* file, simply use *vi* to create one. Enter into this file the set, ab, and map commands that you want to have in effect whenever you use *vi* or *ex*. (ab and map are discussed later in this chapter.) A sample *.exrc* file looks like this:

```
set nowrapscan wrapmargin=7
set sections=SeAhBhChDh nomesg
map q :w^M:n^M
map v dwElp
ab ORA O'Reilly & Associates, Inc.
```

Since the file is actually read by *ex* before it enters visual mode (*vi*), commands in *.exrc* should not have a preceding colon.

Alternate Environments

In addition to reading the *.exrc* file in your home directory, *vi* will read a file called *.exrc* in the current directory. This allows you to set options that are appropriate to a particular project.

For example, you might want to have one set of options in a directory mainly used for programming:

```
set number lisp autoindent sw=4 terse
set tags=/usr/lib/tags
```

and another set of options in a directory used for text editing:

```
set wrapmargin=15 ignorecase
```

Note that you can set certain options in the *.exrc* file in your home directory and unset them in a local directory.

NOTE

In System V, Release 3.2 and later, *vi* doesn't read *.exrc* files in the current directory unless you first set the exrc option in your home directory's *.exrc* file:

```
set exrc
```

This mechanism prevents other people from placing, in your working directory, an *.exrc* file whose commands might jeopardize the security of your system.

You can also define alternate *vi* environments by saving option settings in a file other than *.exrc* and reading in that file with the :so command. For example:

```
:so .progoptions
```

Local *.exrc* files are also useful for defining abbreviations and key mappings (described later in this chapter). When we write a book or manual, we save all abbreviations to be used in that book in an *.exrc* file in the directory in which the book is being created.

Some Useful Options

As you can see when you type :set all, there are an awful lot of options that can be set. Many of them are used internally by *vi* and aren't usually changed. Others are important in certain cases, but not in others (for example, noredraw and window can be useful on a dialup line at a low baud rate). The table in Appendix B, *Setting Environment Options*, contains a brief description of each option. We recommend that you take some time to play with setting options—if an option looks interesting, try setting it (or unsetting it) and watch what happens while you edit. You may find some surprisingly useful tools.

As discussed earlier in this book, one option, wrapmargin, is essential for editing nonprogram text. wrapmargin specifies the size of the right margin that will be used to autowrap text as you type. (This saves manually typing carriage returns.) A typical value is 7 to 15:

```
:set wrapmargin=10
```

Three other options control how *vi* acts when conducting a search. Normally, a search differentiates between uppercase and lowercase (*foo* does not match *Foo*), wraps around to the beginning of the file (meaning that you can begin your search anywhere in the file and still find all occurrences), and recognizes wildcard characters when pattern matching. The default settings that control these options are noignorecase, wrapscan, and magic, respectively. To change any of these defaults, you would set the opposite toggle options: ignorecase, nowrapscan, and nomagic.

Options that may be of particular interest to programmers include: lisp, autoindent, showmatch, tabstop, shiftwidth, number, and list, as well as their opposite toggle options.

Executing UNIX Commands

You can display or read in the results of any UNIX command while you are editing in *vi*. An exclamation mark (!) tells *ex* to create a shell and to regard what follows as a UNIX command:

```
:!command
```

So if you are editing and you want to check the time or date without exiting *vi*, you can enter:

```
:!date
```

The time and date will appear on your screen; press RETURN to continue editing at the same place in your file.

If you want to give several UNIX commands in a row without returning to *vi* editing in between, you can create a shell with the *ex* command:

```
:sh
```

When you want to exit the shell and return to *vi*, press CTRL-D.

You can combine `:read` with a call to UNIX, to read the results of a UNIX command into your file. As a very simple example:

```
:r !date
```

will read in the system's date information into the text of your file. By preceding the `:r` command with a line address, you can read the result of the command in at any desired point in your file. By default, it will appear after the current line.

Suppose you are editing a file and want to read in four phone numbers from a file called *phone*, but in alphabetical order. *phone* reads:

```
Willing, Sue    333-4444
Walsh, Linda    555-6666
Quercia, Valerie   777-8888
Dougherty, Nancy   999-0000
```

The command:

```
:r !sort phone
```

reads in the contents of *phone* after they have been passed through the sort filter:

```
Dougherty, Nancy   999-0000
Quercia, Valerie   777-8888
Walsh, Linda   555-6666
Willing, Sue   333-4444
```

Suppose you are editing a file and want to insert text from another file in the directory, but you can't remember the new file's name. You *could* perform this task the long way: exit your file, give the `ls` command, note the correct filename, reenter your file, and search for your place.

Or you could do the task in fewer steps:

Keystrokes   **Result**

`:!ls`

```
file1           file2           letter
newfile         practice
```

Display list of files in directory. Note correct filename. Press RETURN to continue editing.

`:r newfile`

```
"newfile" 35 lines, 949 characters
```

Read in the new file.

Filtering Text Through a Command

You can also send a block of text as standard input to a UNIX command. The output from this command replaces the block of text in the buffer. You can filter text through a command from either *ex* or *vi*. The main difference between the two methods is that you indicate the block of text with line addresses in *ex* and with text objects (movement commands) in *vi*.

Filtering Text with ex

The first example demonstrates how to filter text with *ex*. Assume that the list of names in the preceding example, instead of being contained in a separate file called *phone*, is already contained in the current file on lines 96 through 99. You simply type the addresses of the lines you want to filter, followed by an exclamation mark and the UNIX command to be executed. For example, the command:

```
:96,99!sort
```

will pass lines 96 through 99 through the *sort* filter and replace those lines with the output of *sort*.

Filtering Text with vi

In *vi* text is filtered through a UNIX command by typing an exclamation mark followed by any of *vi*'s movement keystrokes that indicate a block of text, and then by the UNIX command line to be executed. For example:

```
!)command
```

will pass the next sentence through *command*.

There are a couple of unusual features about how *vi* acts when you use this feature.

- First, the exclamation mark doesn't appear on your screen right away. When you type the keystroke(s) for the text object you want to filter, the exclamation mark appears at the bottom of the screen, *but the character you type to reference the object does not.*

- Second, text blocks must be more than one line, so you can use only the keystrokes that would move more than one line (G, { }, ( ), [[ ]], +, −). To repeat the effect, a number may precede either the exclamation mark or the text object. (For example, both !10+ and 10!+ would indicate the next ten lines.) Objects such as **w** do not work unless enough of them are specified so as to exceed a single line. You can also use a slash (/) followed by a *pattern* and a carriage return to specify the object. This takes the text up to the pattern as input to the command.

- Third, there is a special text object that can be used only with this command syntax: you can specify the current line by entering a second exclamation mark:

```
!!command
```

Remember that either the entire sequence or the text object can be preceded by a number to repeat the effect. For instance, to change lines 96 through 99 as in the above example, you could position the cursor on line 96 and enter either:

```
4!!sort
```

or:

```
!4!sort
```

As another example, assume you have a portion of text in a file that you want to change from lowercase to uppercase letters. You could process that portion with the tr command to change the case. In this example, the second sentence is the block of text that will be filtered to the command.

```
One sentence before.
With a screen editor you can scroll the page
move the cursor, delete lines, insert characters,
and more, while seeing the results of your edits
as you make them.
One sentence after.
```

Keystrokes   **Result**

!)

```
One sentence after.
~
~
~
!_
```

An exclamation mark appears on the last line to prompt you for the UNIX command.

tr ' [a-z]' ' [A-Z]'

```
One sentence before.
WITH A SCREEN EDITOR YOU CAN SCROLL THE PAGE
MOVE THE CURSOR, DELETE LINES, INSERT CHARACTERS,
AND MORE, WHILE SEEING THE RESULTS OF YOUR EDITS
AS YOU MAKE THEM.
One sentence after.
```

Enter the UNIX command and press RETURN. The input is replaced by the output.

To repeat the previous command, the syntax is:

```
! object !
```

It is sometimes useful to send sections of a coded document to *nroff* to be replaced by formatted output. Remember that the "original" input is replaced by the output. Fortunately, if there is a mistake, such as an error message being sent instead of the expected output, you can undo the command and restore the lines.

Saving Commands

Often you type the same long phrases over and over in a file. *vi* and *ex* have a number of different ways of saving long sequences of commands, both in command mode and in insert mode. When you call up one of these saved sequences to execute it, all you do is type a few characters (or even only one), and the entire sequence is executed as if you had entered the whole sequence of commands one by one.

Word Abbreviation

You can define abbreviations that *vi* will automatically expand into the full text whenever you type the abbreviation in insert mode. To define an abbreviation, use the *ex* command:

```
:ab abbr phrase
```

abbr is an abbreviation for the specified *phrase*. The sequence of characters that make up the abbreviation will be expanded in insert mode only if you type it as a full word; *abbr* will not be expanded within a word.

Suppose in the file *practice* you want to enter text that contains a frequently recurring phrase such as a difficult product or company name. The command:

```
:ab imrc International Materials Research Center
```

abbreviates *International Materials Research Center* to the initials *imrc*. Now whenever you type *imrc* in insert mode, *imrc* expands to the full text.

Keystrokes   **Result**

```
ithe imrc
```

```
the International Materials Research Center
```

Abbreviations expand as soon as you press a space, a carriage return, or ESC (returning to command mode). When you are choosing abbreviations, choose combinations of characters that don't ordinarily occur while you are typing text. If you create an abbreviation that ends up expanding in places where you don't want it to, you can disable the abbreviation by typing:

```
:unab abbr
```

To list your currently defined abbreviations, type:

```
:ab
```

The characters that compose your abbreviation cannot also appear at the end of your phrase. For example, if you issue the command:

```
:ab PG This movie is rated PG
```

you'll get the message "No tail recursion," and the abbreviation won't be set. The message means that you have tried to define something that will expand itself repeatedly, creating an infinite loop. If you issue the command:

```
:ab PG the PG rating system
```

you may or may not produce an infinite loop, but in either case you won't get a warning message. For example, when the above command was tested on a System V version of UNIX, the expansion worked. On a Berkeley version, though, the abbreviation expanded repeatedly, like this:

```
the the the the the ...
```

until a memory error occurred and *vi* quit. We recommend that you avoid repeating your abbreviation as part of the defined phrase.

Using the map Command

While you're editing, you may find that you are using a command sequence frequently, or you may occasionally use a very complex command sequence. To save yourself keystrokes, or the time that it takes to remember the sequence, you can assign the sequence to an unused key by using the map command.

The map command acts a lot like ab except that you define a macro for command mode instead of insert mode.

> :map *x sequence* — Define character *x* as a *sequence* of editing commands.
>
> :unmap *x* — Disable the *sequence* defined for *x*.
>
> :map — List the characters that are currently mapped.

Before you can start creating your own maps, you need to know the keys not used in command mode that are available for user-defined commands:

Letters: g K q V v

Control keys: ^A ^K ^O ^T ^W ^X

Symbols: _ * \ =

(Note: The = is used by *vi* if Lisp mode is set.)

Depending on your terminal, you may also be able to associate map sequences with special function keys.

With maps you can create simple or complex command sequences. As a simple example, you could define a command to reverse the order of words. In *vi*, with the cursor as shown:

```
you can the scroll page
```

the sequence to put *the* after *scroll* would be dwelp: delete word, dw; move to the end of next word, e; move one space to the right, 1; put the deleted word there, p. Saving this sequence:

```
:map v dwelp
```

enables you to reverse the order of two words at any time in the editing session with the single keystroke v.

Protecting Keys from Interpretation by ex

Note that when defining a map, you cannot simply type certain keys, such as RETURN, ESC, BACKSPACE, and DELETE as part of the command to be mapped, because these keys already have meaning within *ex*. If you want to include one of these keys as part of the command sequence, you must escape the normal meaning by preceding the key with ^V (CTRL-V). The keystroke ^V appears in the map as the ^ character. Characters following the ^V also do not appear as you expect. For example, a carriage return appears as ^M, escape as ^[, backspace as ^H, and so on.

On the other hand, if you want to use a control character as the character to be mapped, in most cases all you have to do is hold down the CTRL key and press the letter key at the same time. So, for example, all you need to do in order to map ^A is to type:

```
:map CTRL-A sequence
```

There are, however, three control characters that must be escaped with a ^V. They are ^T, ^W, and ^X. So, for example, if you want to map ^T, you must type:

```
:map CTRL-V CTRL-T sequence
```

The use of CTRL-V applies to any *ex* command, not just a map command. This means that you can type a carriage return in an abbreviation or a substitution command. For example, the abbreviation:

```
:ab 123 one^Mtwo^Mthree
```

expands to this:

```
one
two
three
```

(Here we show the sequence CTRL-V RETURN as ^M, the way it would appear on your screen.)

You can also globally add lines at certain locations. The command:

```
:g/^Section/s//As you recall, in^M&/
```

inserts, before all lines beginning with the word *Section*, a phrase on a separate line. The & restores the search pattern.

Unfortunately, one character always has special meaning in *ex* commands, even if you try to quote it with CTRL-V . Recall that the vertical bar (|) has special meaning as a separator of multiple *ex* commands. You cannot use a vertical bar in insert mode maps.

Now that you've seen how to use CTRL-V to protect certain keys inside *ex* commands, you're ready to define some powerful map sequences.

Complex Mapping Example

Assume that you have a glossary with entries like this:

```
map - an ex command which allows you to associate
a complex command sequence with a single key.
```

You would like to convert this glossary list to *nroff* format, so that it looks like this:

```
.IP "map" 10n
An ex command...
```

The best way to define a complex map is to do the edit once manually, writing down each keystroke that you must type. Then recreate these keystrokes as a map. You want to:

1. Insert the ms macro for an indented paragraph at the beginning of the line. Insert the first quotation mark as well (I.IP ").

2. Press ESC to terminate insert mode.

3. Move to the end of the first word (e) and add a second quotation mark, followed by a space and the size of the indent (a" 10n).

4. Press RETURN to insert a new line.

5. Press ESC to terminate insert mode.

6. Remove the hyphen and two surrounding spaces (3x) and capitalize the next word (~).

That's quite an editing chore if you have to repeat it more than a few times. With :map you can save the entire sequence so that it can be re-executed with a single keystroke:

```
:map g I.IP "^[ea" 10n^M^[3x~
```

Note that you have to "quote" both the ESC and RETURN characters with CTRL-V . ^[is the sequence that appears when you type CTRL-V followed by [ESC]. ^M is the sequence shown when you type [CTRL-V] [RETURN].

Now, simply typing g will perform the entire series of edits. At a slow baud rate you can actually see the edits happening individually. At a fast baud rate it will seem to happen by magic.

Don't be discouraged if your first attempt at key mapping fails. A small error in defining the map can give very different results from the ones you expect. Type u to undo the edit, and try again.

More Examples of Mapping Keys

The examples below will give you an idea of the clever shortcuts possible when defining keyboard maps.

1. Add text whenever you move to the end of a word:

   ```
   :map e ea
   ```

   Most of the time, the only reason you want to move to the end of a word is to add text. This map sequence puts you in insert mode automatically. Note that the mapped key, e, has meaning in *vi*. You're allowed to map a key that is already used by *vi*, but the key's normal function will be unavailable as long as the map is in effect. This isn't so bad in this case, since the E command is often identical to e.

2. Transpose two words:

   ```
   :map K dwElp
   ```

   We discussed this sequence earlier in the chapter, but now you need to use E (assume here, and in the remaining examples, that the e command is mapped to ea). Remember that the cursor begins on the first of the two words. Unfortunately, because of the l command, this sequence (and the earlier version) doesn't work if the two words are at the end of a line: during the sequence, the cursor ends up at the end of the line, and l cannot move further right. Here's a better solution:

   ```
   :map K dwwP
   ```

You could also use W instead of w.

3. Save a file and edit the next one in a series:

```
:map q :w^M:n^M
```

Notice that you can map keys to *ex* commands, but be sure to finish each *ex* command with a carriage return. This sequence makes it easy to move from one file to the next and is useful when you've opened many short files with one *vi* command. Mapping the letter q helps you remember that the sequence is similar to a "quit."

4. Put *troff* emboldening codes around a word:

```
:map v i\fB^[e\fP^[
```

This sequence assumes that the cursor is at the beginning of the word. First, you enter insert mode, then you type the code for bold font. In map commands, you don't need to type two backslashes to produce one backslash. Next, you return to command mode by typing a "quoted" ESC . Finally, you append the closing *troff* code at the end of the word, and you return to command mode. Notice that when we appended to the end of the word, we didn't need to use e a, since this sequence is itself mapped to the single letter e. This shows you that map sequences are allowed to contain other map commands. (The ability to use nested map sequences is controlled by *vi*'s remap option, which is normally enabled.)

5. Put *troff* emboldening codes around a word, even when the cursor is not at the beginning of the word:

```
:map V lbi\fB^[e\fP^[
```

This sequence is the same as the previous one, except that it uses lb to handle the additional task of positioning the cursor at the beginning of the word. The cursor might be in the middle of the word, so you want to move to the beginning with the b command.

But if the cursor were already at the beginning of the word, the b command would move the cursor to the previous word instead. To guard against that case, type an l before moving back with b, so that the cursor never starts on the first letter of the word. You can define variations of this sequence by replacing the b with B and the e with Ea. In all cases, though, the l command prevents this sequence from working if the cursor is at the end of a line. (You could append a space to get around this.)

6. Repeatedly find and remove parentheses from around a word or phrase:*

```
:map = xf)xn
```

This sequence assumes that you first found an open parenthesis, by typing / (followed by RETURN.

If you choose to remove the parentheses, then use the map command: delete the open parenthesis with x, find the closing one with f), delete it with x, and then repeat your search for an open parenthesis with n.

If you don't want to remove the parentheses (for example, if they're being used correctly), then don't use the map command: press n instead to find the next open parenthesis.

You could also modify the map sequence above to handle matching pairs of quotes.

7. Place C comments around an entire line:

```
:map g I/* ^[A */^[
```

This sequence inserts /* at the line's beginning and appends */ at the line's end. You could also map a substitute command to do the same thing:

```
:map g :s/.*/\/* & *\//^M
```

Here, you match the entire line (with .*), and when you replay it (with &), you surround the line with the comment symbols. Note that you have to escape the / in the comment.

8. Safely repeat a long insertion:

```
:map ^J :set wm=0^M.:set wm=10^M
```

We mentioned in Chapter 2, *Simple Editing*, that *vi* occasionally has difficulty repeating long insertions of text when wrapmargin is set. This map command is a useful workaround. It temporarily turns off the wrapmargin (by setting to 0), gives the repeat command, and then restores the wrapmargin. Note that a map sequence can combine *ex* and *vi* commands.

---

* From the article by Walter Zintz, in *UNIX World*, April 1990.

In the previous example, even though ˆJ is a *vi* command (it moves the cursor down a line), this key is safe to map because it's really the same as the j command. There are many keys that either perform the same tasks as other keys or that are rarely used. However, you should be familiar with the *vi* commands before you boldly disable their normal use by using them in map definitions.

Mapping Keys for Insert Mode

Normally, maps apply only to command mode—after all, in insert mode, keys stand for themselves and shouldn't be mapped as commands. However, by adding an exclamation mark (!) to the map command, you can force it to override the ordinary meaning of a key and produce the map in insert mode. This feature is useful when you find yourself in insert mode but need to escape briefly to command mode, run a command, and then return to insert mode.

For example, suppose you just typed a word but forgot to italicize it (or place quotes around it, etc.). You can define this map:

```
:map! + ˆ[bi\fIˆ[ea\fP
```

Now, when you type a + at the end of a word, you will surround the word with *troff* italicization codes. The + won't show up in the text.

The sequence above escapes to command mode (ˆ[), backs up to insert the first code (bi\fI), escapes again (ˆ[), and moves ahead to append the second code (ea\fP). Since the map sequence begins and ends in insert mode, you can continue entering text after italicizing the word.

Here's another example. Suppose that you've been typing your text, and you realize that the previous line should have ended with a colon. You can correct that by defining this map sequence:*

```
:map! % ˆ[kA:ˆ[jA
```

Now, if you type a % anywhere along your current line, you'll append a colon to the end of the previous line. This command escapes to command mode, moves up a line, and appends the colon (ˆ[kA:).

---

* From the article by Walter Zintz, in *UNIX World*, April 1990.

The command then escapes again, moves down to the line you were on, and leaves you in insert mode (˄ [jA).

Note that we wanted to use uncommon characters (% and +) for the previous map commands. When a character is mapped for insert mode, you can no longer type that character as text. To reinstate a character for normal typing, use the command:

```
:unmap! x
```

where *x* is the character that was previously mapped for insert mode.

Insert-mode mapping is often more appropriate for tying character strings to special keys that you wouldn't otherwise use. It is especially useful with programmable function keys.

Mapping Function Keys

Many terminals have programmable function keys. You can usually set up these keys to print whatever character or characters you want using a special setup mode on the terminal. However, keys programmed using a terminal's setup mode only work on that terminal; they may also limit the action of programs that want to set up those function keys themselves.

ex allows you to map function keys by number, using the syntax:

```
:map #1 commands
```

for function key number 1, and so on. (It can do this because the editor has access to the entry for that terminal found in either the *termcap* or *terminfo* database and knows the escape sequence normally put out by the function key.)

As with other keys, maps apply by default to command mode, but by using the map! commands as well, you can define two separate values for a function key—one to be used in command mode, the other in insert mode. For example, if you are a *troff* user, you might want to put font-switch codes on function keys. For example:

```
:map #1 i\fI˄[
:map! #1 \fI
```

If you are in command mode, the first function key will enter insert mode, type in the three characters \fI, and return to command mode.

If you are already in insert mode, the key will simply type the three-character *troff* code.

NOTE

> If function keys have been redefined in the terminal's setup mode, the #*n* syntax might not work since the function keys no longer put out the expected control or escape sequence as described in its terminal database entry. You will need to examine the *termcap* entry (or *terminfo* source) for your terminal and check the definitions for the function keys. In addition, there are some terminals whose function keys perform only local actions and don't actually send any characters to the computer. Such function keys can't be mapped.

The terminal capabilities k1, k2 through k0 describe the first ten function keys. The capabilities l1, l2 through l0 describe the remaining function keys. Using your terminal's setup mode, you can change the control or escape sequence output by the function key to correspond with the *termcap* or *terminfo* entry. (For more information, see the Nutshell Handbook *termcap & terminfo*.)

If the sequence contains ^M, which is a carriage return, press CTRL-M. For instance, in order to have function key 1 available for mapping, the terminal database entry for your terminal must have a definition of k1, such as:

```
k1=^A@^M
```

In turn, the definition:

```
^A@^M
```

must be what is output when you press that key.

To test what the function key puts out, press the key at the UNIX prompt, followed by a RETURN, if necessary. The shell should display the sequence output by the function key after trying unsuccessfully to execute it as a UNIX command.

Mapping Other Special Keys

Many keyboards have special keys, such as HOME, END, PAGE UP, and PAGE DOWN, that duplicate commands in *vi*. If the terminal's *termcap* or *terminfo* description is complete, *vi* will be able to recognize these keys. But if it isn't, you can use the map command to make them available to *vi*. These keys generally send an escape sequence to the computer—an escape character followed by a string of one or more other characters. In order to trap the escape, you should press ^V before pressing the special key in the map. For example, to map the HOME key on the keyboard of an IBM PC to a reasonable *vi* equivalent, you might define the following map:

```
:map CTRL-V HOME    1G
```

This appears on your screen as:

```
:map ^[[H 1G
```

Similar map commands display as follows:

```
:map CTRL-V END     G        displays    :map ^[[Y G
:map CTRL-V PAGE UP      ^F   displays    :map ^[[V ^F
:map CTRL-V PAGE DOWN      ^B displays    :map ^[[U ^B
```

You'll probably want to place these maps in your *.exrc* file. Note that if a special key generates a long escape sequence (containing multiple non-printing characters), ^V quotes only the initial escape character, and the map doesn't work. You will have to find the entire escape sequence (perhaps from the terminal manual) and type it in manually, quoting at the appropriate points, rather than simply pressing ^V and then the key.

@-Functions

Named buffers provide yet another way to create "macros"—complex command sequences that you can repeat with only a few keystrokes.

If you type a command line in your text (either a *vi* sequence or an *ex* command *preceded by a colon*), then delete it into a named buffer, you can execute the contents of that buffer with the @ command. For example, open a new line and enter:

```
cwgadfly CTRL-V ESC
```

This will appear as:

```
cwgadfly^[
```

on your screen. Press ESC again to exit insert mode, then delete the line into buffer g by typing "gdd. Now, whenever you place the cursor at the beginning of a word and type @g, that word in your text will be changed to *gadfly*.

Since @ is interpreted as a *vi* command, a dot (.) will repeat the entire sequence, even if the buffer contains an *ex* command. @@ repeats the last @, and u or U can be used to undo the effect of @.

This is a simple example. @-functions are useful because they can be adapted to very specific commands. They are especially useful when you are editing between files, because you can store the commands in their named buffers and access them from any file you edit. @-functions are also useful in combination with the global replacement commands discussed in Chapter 6, *Global Replacement*.

Using ex Scripts

Certain *ex* commands you use only within *vi*, such as maps, abbreviations, and so on. If you store these commands in a separate file called *.exrc*, the commands will automatically be executed when you invoke *vi*. Any file that contains commands to execute is called a *script*.

The commands in a typical *.exrc* script are of no use outside *vi*. However, you can save other *ex* commands in a script, and then execute the script on a file or on multiple files. Mostly you'll use substitute commands in these external scripts.

For a writer, a useful application of *ex* scripts is to ensure consistency of terminology—or even of spelling— across a document set. For example, let's assume that you've run the UNIX spell command on two files and that the command has printed out the following list of misspellings:

```
$ spell sect1 sect2
chmod
ditroff
myfile
thier
writeable
```

As is often the case, `spell` has flagged a few technical terms and special cases it doesn't recognize, but it has also identified two genuine spelling errors.

Because we checked two files at once, we don't know which files the errors occurred in or where they are in the files. Although there are ways to find this out, and the job wouldn't be too hard for only two errors in two files, you can easily imagine how time consuming the job could grow for a poor speller or for a typist proofing many files at once.

To make the job easier, you could write an *ex* script containing the following commands:

```
g/thier/s//their/g
g/writeable/s//writable/g
wq
```

Assume you've saved these lines in a file named *exscript*. The script could be executed from within *vi* with the command:

```
:so exscript
```

or the script can be applied to a file right from the command line. Then you could edit the files *sect1* and *sect2* as follows:

```
$ ex - sect1 < exscript
$ ex - sect2 < exscript
```

(The minus sign following the invocation of *ex* tells it to accept its commands from standard input.)

If the script were longer than the one in our simple example, we would already have saved a fair amount of time. However, you might wonder if there isn't some way to avoid repeating the process for each file to be edited. Sure enough, we can write a shell script that includes, but generalizes, the invocation of *ex*, so that it can be used on any number of files:

Looping in a Shell Script

If you don't already know this, it's about time you learned that the shell is a programming language as well as a command-line interpreter. To invoke *ex* on a number of files, we use a simple type of shell script command called the `for` loop. A `for` loop allows you to apply a sequence of commands for each argument given to the script. (The `for` loop is probably the single most useful piece of shell programming for beginners. You'll want to remember it even if you don't write any other shell programs.)

Here's the syntax of a `for` loop:

```
for variable in list
do
      command(s)
done
```

For example:

```
for file in $*
do
      ex - $file < exscript
done
```

(The command doesn't need to be indented; we indented it for clarity.) After we create this shell script, we save it in a file called *correct* and make it executable with the chmod command. (If you aren't familiar with the chmod command and the procedures for adding a command to your UNIX search path, see the Nutshell Handbook *Learning the UNIX Operating System.*) Now we can simply type:

```
$ correct sect1 sect2
```

The `for` loop in *correct* will assign each argument (each file in the list specified by `$*`, which stands for *all arguments*) to the variable *file* and execute the *ex* script on the contents of that variable.

It may be easier to grasp how the `for` loop works with an example whose output is more visible. Let's look at a script to rename files:

```
for file in $*
do
      mv $file $file.x
done
```

Assuming this script is in an executable file called *move*, here's what we can do:

```
$ ls
ch01 ch02 ch03 move
$ move ch??
$ ls
ch01.x ch02.x ch03.x move
```

With a little creativity, you could rewrite the script to rename the files more specifically:

```
for nn in $*
do
      mv ch$nn sect$nn
done
```

With the script written this way, you'd specify numbers instead of filenames on the command line:

```
$ ls
ch01 ch02 ch03 move
$ move 01 02 03
$ ls
sect01 sect02 sect03 move
```

The `for` loop need not take `$*` (all arguments) as the list of values to be substituted. You can specify an explicit list as well; for example:

```
for variable in a b c d
```

will assign *variable* to *a*, *b*, *c*, and *d* in turn. Or you can substitute the output of a command; for example:

```
for variable in `grep -l "Alcuin"`
```

will assign *variable* in turn to the name of each file in which `grep` finds the string *Alcuin*.

If no list is specified:

```
for variable
```

the variable will be assigned to each command-line argument in turn, much as it was in our initial example. This is actually not equivalent to:

```
for variable in $*
```

but to:

```
for variable in $@
```

which has a slightly different meaning. The symbol $* expands to *$1*, *$2*, *$3*, etc., but $@ expands to *"$1"*, *"$2"*, *"$3"*, etc. Quotation marks prevent further interpretation of special characters.

Let's return to our main point and our original script:

```
for file in $*
do
      ex - $file < exscript
done
```

It may seem a little inelegant to have to use two scripts—the shell script and the *ex* script. And in fact, the shell does provide a way to include an editing script inside a shell script.

Here Documents

In a shell script, the operator << means to take the following lines, up to a specified string, as input to a command. (This is often called a *here document*.) Using this syntax, we could include our editing commands in *correct* like this:

```
for file in $*
do
ex - $file << end-of-script
g/thier/s//their/g
g/writeable/s//writable/g
wq
end-of-script
done
```

The string *end-of-script* is entirely arbitrary—it just needs to be a string that won't otherwise appear in the input and can be used by the shell to recognize when the here document is finished. By convention, many users specify the end of a here document with the string *EOF*, or *E_O_F*, to indicate the end of the file.

There are advantages and disadvantages to each approach shown. If you want to make a one-time series of edits and don't mind rewriting the script each time, the here document provides an effective way to do the job.

However, it's more flexible to write the editing commands in a separate file from the shell script. For example, you could establish the convention that you will always put editing commands in a file called *exscript*. Then you only need to write the *correct* script once. You can store it away in your personal "tools" directory (which you've added to your search path) and use it whenever you like.

Sorting Text Blocks: A Sample ex Script

Suppose you want to alphabetize a file of *nroff*-encoded glossary definitions. Each term begins with an .IP macro. In addition, each entry is surrounded by the .KS/.KE macro pair. (This ensures that the term and its definition will print as a block and will not be split across a new page.) The glossary file looks something like this:

```
.KS
.IP "TTY_ARGV" 2n
The command, specified as an argument vector,
that the TTY subwindow executes.
.KE
.KS
.IP "ICON_IMAGE" 2n
Sets or gets the remote image for icon's image.
.KE
.KS
.IP "XV_LABEL" 2n
Specifies a frame's header or an icon's label.
.KE
.KS
.IP "SERVER_SYNC" 2n
Synchronizes with the server once.
Does not set synchronous mode.
.KE
```

You can alphabetize a file by running the lines through the UNIX `sort` command, but you don't really want to sort every line. You want to sort only the glossary terms, moving each definition— untouched—along with its corresponding term. As it turns out, you can treat each text block as a unit by joining the block into one line. Here's the first version of your *ex* script:

```
g/\.KS/,/\.KE/j
%!sort
```

Each glossary entry is found between a .KS and .KE macro. `j` is the *ex* command to join a line (the equivalent in *vi* is J). So, the first command joins every glossary entry into one "line." The second command then sorts the file, producing lines like this:

```
.KS .IP "ICON_IMAGE" 2n Sets or gets ... image. .KE
.KS .IP "SERVER_SYNC" 2n Synchronizes with ... mode. .KE
.KS .IP "TTY_ARGV" 2n The command, ... executes. .KE
.KS .IP "XV_LABEL" 2n Specifies a ... icon's label. .KE
```

The lines are now sorted by glossary entry; unfortunately, each line also has macros and text mixed in (we've used ellipses (...) to show omitted text). Somehow, you need to insert carriage returns to "un-join" the lines. You can do this by modifying your *ex* script: mark the joining points of the text blocks *before* you join them, and then replace the markers with carriage returns. Here's the expanded *ex* script:

```
g/\.KS/,/\.KE/-1s/$/@@/
g/\.KS/,/\.KE/j
%!sort
%s/@@ /^M/g
```

The first three commands produce lines like this:

```
.KS@@ .IP "ICON_IMAGE" 2n@@ Sets or gets ... image. @@ .KE
.KS@@ .IP "SERVER_SYNC" 2n@@ Synchronizes with ... mode. @@ .KE
.KS@@ .IP "TTY_ARGV" 2n@@ The ... vector, @@ that ... .@@ .KE
.KS@@ .IP "XV_LABEL" 2n@@ Specifies a ... icon's label. @@ .KE
```

Note the extra space following the @@. The spaces result from the j command, because it converts each carriage return into a space.

The first command marks the original line breaks with @@. You don't need to mark the end of the block (after the .KE), so the first command uses a −1 to move back up one line at the end of each block. The fourth command restores the line breaks by replacing the markers (plus the extra space) with carriage returns. Now, your file is sorted by blocks.

Comments in ex Scripts

You may want to reuse such a script, adapting it to a new situation. With a complex script like this, it is wise to add comments so that it's easier for someone else (or even yourself!) to reconstruct how it works. In *ex* scripts, anything following a double quote is ignored during execution, so a double quote can mark the beginning of a comment. Comments can go on their own line. They can also go at the end of any command that doesn't interpret a quote as part of the command. (For example, a quote has meaning to map commands and shell escapes, so you can't end such lines with a comment.)

Besides using comments, you can specify a command by its full name, something that would ordinarily be too time consuming from within *vi*. Finally, if you add spaces, the *ex* script above becomes this more readable one:

```
" Mark lines between each KS/KE block
global /\.KS/,/\.KE/-1 substitute /$/@@/
" Now join the blocks into one line
global /\.KS/,/\.KE/ join
" Sort each block--now really one line each
%!sort
" Restore the joined lines to original blocks
% substitute /@@ /^M/g
```

ex Scripts Built by diff

A further example of the use of *ex* scripts is built into a UNIX program called `diff`, which compares two files and prints out lines that differ. The −e option of `diff` produces an editing script usable with either *ed* or *ex*, instead of the usual output. This script consists of a sequence of a (add), c (change), and d (delete) commands necessary to recreate *file1* from *file2* (the first and second files specified on the `diff` command line).

Obviously there is no need to completely recreate the first file from the second, because you could do that easily with cp. However, by editing the script produced by `diff`, you can come up with some desired combination of the two versions.

It might take you a moment to think of a case in which you might have use for this feature. Consider this one: two people have unknowingly made edits to different copies of a file, and you need the two versions merged. (This can happen especially easily in a networked environment, in which people copy files between machines. Poor coordination can easily result in this kind of problem.)

To make this situation concrete, let's take a look at two versions of the same paragraph, which we want to combine:

```
Version 1:
The Book of Kells,
now one of the treasures of the Trinity College Library
in Dublin,
was found in the ancient monastery at Ceannanus Mor,
now called Kells.
It is a beautifully illustrated manuscript of the Latin
Gospels, and also contains notes on local history.
It was written in the eighth century.
The manuscript is generally regarded as the finest
example of Celtic illumination.

Version 2:
The Book of Kells
was found in the ancient monastery at Ceannanus Mor,
now called Kells.
It is a beautifully illustrated manuscript of the Latin
Gospels, and also contains notes on local history.
It is believed to have been written in the eighth century.
The manuscript is generally regarded as the finest
example of Celtic illumination.
```

As you can see, there is one additional phrase in each of the two files. We can merge them into one file that incorporates both edits. Typing:

```
$ diff -e version1 version2 > exscript
```

will yield the following output in the file *exscript*:

```
8c
It is believed to have been written in the eighth century.
.
1,3c
The Book of Kells
.
```

You'll notice that the script appears in reverse order, with the changes later in the file appearing first. This is essential whenever you're making changes based on line numbers; otherwise, changes made earlier in the file may change the numbering, rendering the later parts of the script ineffective. You'll also notice that, as mentioned, this script will simply recreate *version1*, which is not what we want. We want the change to line 8, but not the change to lines 1 through 3. We want to edit the script so that it looks like this:

```
8c
It is believed to have been written in the eighth century.
.
w
```

(Notice that we had to add the **w** command to write the results of the edit back into the file.) Now we can type:

```
$ ex - version1 < exscript
```

to get the resulting merged file:

```
The Book of Kells,
now one of the treasures of the Trinity College Library
in Dublin,
was found in the ancient monastery at Ceannanus Mor,
now called Kells.
It is a beautifully illustrated manuscript of the Latin
Gospels, and also contains notes on local history.
It is believed to have been written in the eighth century.
The manuscript is generally regarded as the finest
example of Celtic illumination.
```

Using **diff** like this can get confusing, especially when there are many changes. It is easy to get the direction of changes confused or to make the wrong edits. Just remember to do the following:

- Specify the file that is closest in content to your eventual target as the first file on the **diff** command line. This will minimize the size of the editing script that is produced.

- After you have corrected the editing script so that it makes only the changes that you want, apply it to that same file (the first file).

Nonetheless, because there is so much room for error, it is better not to have your script write the changes back directly into one of your source files. Instead of adding a **w** command at the end of the script, add the command %p (or 1, $p) to write the results to standard output. This is almost always preferable when you are using a complex editing script.

If we use this command in the editing script, the command line to actually make the edits would look like this:

```
$ ex - version1 < exscript > version3
```

Writers often find themselves making extensive changes and then wishing they could go back and recover some part of an earlier version. Obviously, frequent backups will help. However, if backup storage space is at a premium, it is possible (though a little awkward) to save only some older version of a file, and then keep incremental **diff -e** scripts to mark the differences between each successive version.

To apply multiple scripts to a single file, you can simply pipe them to *ex* rather than redirecting input:

```
$ cat script1 script2 script3 | ex - oldfile
```

But wait! How do you get your w (or %p) command into the pipeline? You could edit the last script to include one of these commands. But there's another trick that we ought to look at because it illustrates another useful feature of the shell that many people are unaware of. If you enclose a semicolon-separated list of commands in parentheses, the standard output of all of the commands are combined, and can be redirected together. The immediate application is that, if you type:

```
$ cat script1 script2 script3; echo '%p' | ex - oldfile
```

the results of the `cat` command will be sent, as usual, to standard output, and only the results of `echo` will be piped to *ex*. But if you type:

```
$ (cat script1 script2 script3; echo '%p') | ex -oldfile
```

the output of the entire sequence will make it into the pipeline, which is what we want.

Where to Go from Here

If this discussion has whetted your appetite for even more editing power, you should be aware that UNIX provides editors even more powerful than *ex*: the *sed* stream editor and the *awk* data manipulation language. For information on these programs, see the Nutshell Handbook *Sed & Awk*.

Editing Program Source Code

All of the features discussed so far in this book are of interest whether you are editing English text or program source code. However, there are a number of additional features that are of interest chiefly to programmers. These include indentation control, searching for the beginning and end of procedures, and using `ctags`.

The following discussion is adapted from documentation provided by Mortice Kern Systems with their excellent implementation of *vi* for DOS-based systems, available as a part of the MKS Toolkit or separately as MKS Vi. It is reprinted by permission of Mortice Kern Systems.

Indentation Control

The source code for a program differs from ordinary text in a number of ways. One of the most important of these is the way in which source code uses indentation. Indentation shows the logical structure of the program: the way in which statements are grouped into blocks.

vi provides automatic indentation control. To use it, issue the command:

```
:set autoindent
```

Now, when you indent a line with spaces or tabs, the following lines will automatically be indented by the same amount. When you press [RETURN] after typing the first indented line, the cursor goes to the next line and automatically indents the same distance as the previous line.

As a programmer, you will find this saves you quite a bit of work getting the indentation right, especially when you have several levels of indentation.

When you are entering code with autoindent enabled, typing [CTRL-T] at the start of a line gives you another level of indentation and typing [CTRL-D] takes one away.

We should point out that [CTRL-T] and [CTRL-D] are typed while you are in insert mode, unlike most other commands, which are typed in command mode.

The amount of indentation provided by [CTRL-T] or >> is one tab character. Tab stops are set every eight spaces by default. A command like:

```
:set tabstop=4
```

will change the tab settings for a file.

Try using the autoindent option when you are entering source code. It simplifies the job of getting indentation correct. It can even sometimes help you avoid bugs (e.g., in C source code, where you usually need one closing curly brace (}) for every level of indentation you go backwards).

The << and >> commands are also helpful when indenting source code. By default, >> shifts a line right eight spaces (i.e., adds eight spaces of indentation) and << shifts a line left eight spaces. For example, move the cursor to the beginning of this line and press the > key twice (>>). You will see the line move right. If you now press the < key twice (<<), the line will move back again.

You can shift a number of lines by typing the number followed by >> or <<. For example, move the cursor to the first line of this paragraph and type 5>>. You will shift all five lines in the paragraph.

The default shift is eight spaces (right or left). This default can be changed with a command like:

```
:set shiftwidth=4
```

You will find it convenient to have a shiftwidth that is the same size as the width between tab stops.

Sometimes indentation won't work the way you expect, because what you believe to be a tab character is actually one or more spaces. Normally, your screen displays both a tab and a space as white space, making the two indistinguishable. You can, however, issue the command:

```
:set list
```

This alters your display so that a tab appears as the control character ^I and an end-of-line appears as a $. This way, you can spot a true space, and you can see extra spaces at the end of a line. A temporary equivalent is the :l command. For example, the command:

```
:5,20 l
```

displays lines 5 through 20, showing tab characters and end-of-line characters.

A Special Search Command

The characters (, [, {, and < can all be called opening brackets. When the cursor is resting on one of these characters, pressing the % key moves the cursor from the opening bracket forward to the corresponding closing bracket—),], }, or >—keeping in mind the usual rules for nesting brackets. For example, if you were to move the cursor to the first (in:

```
if ( cos(a[i]) > sin(b[i]+c[i]) )
{
printf("cos and sin equal!");
}
```

and press %, you would see that the cursor jumps to the parenthesis at the end of the line. This is the closing parenthesis that matches the opening one.

Similarly if the cursor is on one of the closing bracket characters, pressing % will move the cursor backwards to the corresponding opening bracket character. For example, move the cursor to the closing brace bracket after the printf line above and press %.

Not only does this search character help you move forward and backward through a program in long jumps, it lets you check the nesting of brackets and parentheses in source code. For example, if you put the cursor on the first { at the beginning of a C function, pressing % should move you to the } that (you think) ends the function. If it doesn't, something has gone wrong somewhere.

Another technique for searching matching brackets is to turn on the following option:

```
:set showmatch
```

Unlike %, setting showmatch (or its abbreviation sm) helps you while you're in insert mode. When you type a) or a }, the cursor will briefly move back to the matching (or { before returning to your current position.

Using Tags

The source code for a large C program will usually be spread over several files. Sometimes, it is difficult to keep track of which file contains which function definitions. To simplify matters, a command called ctags can be used together with the :tag command of *vi*.

NOTE

This section is of interest to C programmers, but not to those working in other languages.

The `ctags` command is issued at the UNIX command line. Its purpose is to create an information file that *vi* can use later to determine which files define which functions. By default, this file is called *tags*. From within *vi*, a command of the form:

```
:!ctags file.c
```

will create a file named *tags* under your current directory that contains information on the functions defined in *file.c*. A command like:

```
:!ctags *.c
```

will create a *tags* file describing all the C source files under the directory.

Now suppose your *tags* file contains information on all the source files that make up a C program. Also suppose that you want to look at or edit a function in the program but do not know where the function is. From within *vi*, the command:

```
:tag name
```

will look at the *tags* file to find out which file contains the definition of the function *name*. It will then read in the file and position the cursor on the line where the name is defined. In this way, you don't have to know which file you have to edit; you only have to decide which function you want to edit.

NOTE

If you try to use the `:tag` command to read in a new file and you haven't saved your current text since the last time you changed it, *vi* will not let you go to the new file. You must either write out your current file with the `:w` command and then issue `:tag`, or else type:

```
:tag! name
```

to override *vi*'s reluctance to discard edits.

Quick Reference
Movement Commands
Editing Commands
Exit Commands
Command Line Options
Other ex Commands

This appendix lists *vi* commands and *ex* commands according to their use.

Movement Commands

Character	
h, j, k, l	Left, down, up, right ($\leftarrow, \downarrow, \uparrow, \rightarrow$)
Text	
w, W, b, B	Forward, backward by word
e, E	End of word
), (	Beginning of next, previous sentence
}, {	Beginning of next, previous paragraph
]], [[	Beginning of next, previous section
Lines	
0, $	First, last position of current line
^	First character of current line (ignore spaces)
+, −	First character of next, previous line
n |	Column *n* of current line
H	Top line of screen
M	Middle line of screen
L	Last line of screen
*n*H	*n* (number) of lines after top line
*n*L	*n* (number) of lines before last line
Screens	
CTRL-F, CTRL-B	Scroll forward, backward one screen
CTRL-D, CTRL-U	Scroll down, up one-half screen
CTRL-E, CTRL-Y	Show one more line at bottom, top of window
z RETURN	Reposition line with cursor: to top of screen
z .	Reposition line with cursor: to middle of screen
z −	Reposition line with cursor: to bottom of screen
CTRL-L, CTRL-R	Redraw screen (without scrolling)

Movement Commands (continued)

Searches	
`pattern`	Search forward for pattern
`?pattern`	Search backward for pattern
`n, N`	Repeat last search in same, opposite direction
`/, ?`	Repeat previous search forward, backward
`f`*x*	Search forward for character *x* in current line
`F`*x*	Search backward for character *x* in current line
`t`*x*	Search forward for character before *x* in current line
`T`*x*	Search backward for character after *x* in current line
`;`	Repeat previous current-line search
`'`	Repeat previous current-line search in opposite direction
Line number	
CTRL-G	Display current line number
n`G`	Move to line number *n*
`G`	Move to last line in file
`:`*n*	Move to line number *n*
Marking position	
`m`*x*	Mark current position as *x*
`` ` ``*x*	Move cursor to *x*
`` `` ``	Return to previous mark or context
`'`*x*	Move to beginning of line containing mark *x*
`''`	Return to beginning of line containing previous mark

Editing Commands

Insert	
i, a	Insert text before, after cursor
I, A	Insert text at beginning, end of line
o, O	Open new line for text below, above cursor

Change	
r	Change character
cw	Change word
cc	Change current line
C	Change to end of line
R	Type over characters
s	Delete character and substitute text
S	Delete current line and substitute text

Delete, move	
x	Delete character
X	Delete character before cursor
dw	Delete word
dd	Delete current line
D	Delete to end of line
p, P	Put deleted text after, before cursor
"*n*p	Put text from delete buffer number *n* after cursor (for last nine deletions)

Yank	
yw	Yank (copy) word
yy	Yank current line
"ayy	Yank current line into named buffer *a*
p, P	Put yanked text after, before cursor
"aP	Put text from buffer *a* before cursor

Other commands	
.	Repeat last edit command
u, U	Undo last edit; restore current line
J	Join two lines

Editing Commands (continued)

ex edit commands	
`:d`	Delete lines
`:m`	Move lines
`:co` or `:t`	Copy lines
`:.,$d`	Delete from current line to end of file
`:30,60m0`	Move lines 30 through 60 to top of file
`:.,/pattern/co$`	Copy from current line through line containing *pattern* to end of file

Exit Commands

`ZZ`	Write (save) and quit file
`:x`	Write (save) and quit file
`:wq`	Write (save) and quit file
`:w`	Write (save) file
`:w!`	Write (save) file (overriding protection)
`:30,60w newfile`	Write from line 30 through line 60 as *newfile*
`:30,60w>> file`	Write from line 30 through line 60 and append to *file*
`:w %.new`	Write current buffer named *file* as *file.new*
`:q`	Quit file
`:q!`	Quit file (overriding protection)
`Q`	Quit *vi* and invoke *ex*
`:e file2`	Edit *file2* without leaving *vi*
`:n`	Edit next file
`:e!`	Return to version of current file at time of last write (save)
`:e#`	Edit alternate file
`%`	Current filename
`#`	Alternate filename

Command Line Options

vi *file*	Invoke *vi* editor on *file*
vi *file1 file2*	Invoke *vi* editor on files sequentially
view *file*	Invoke *vi* editor on *file* in read-only mode
vi -R *file*	Invoke *vi* editor on *file* in read-only mode
vi -r *file*	Recover *file* and recent edits after system crash
vi + *file*	Open *file* at last line
vi +*n file*	Open *file* directly at line number *n*
vi +/*pattern file*	Open *file* directly at *pattern*
ex *file*	Invoke *ex* editor on *file* from UNIX

Other ex Commands

*Abbreviations**	
:map *x sequence*	Define keystroke *x* as a command *sequence*
:map! *x sequence*	Define *x* as command *sequence* for insert mode
:unmap *x*	Disable the map *x*
:unmap! *x*	Disable insert mode map *x*
:ab *abbr phrase*	Abbreviate *phrase* as *abbr*; when *abbr* is typed in insert mode, it expands to full words or phrases
:unab *abbr*	Disable abbreviation
*Customizing environment:**	
:set *option*	Activate *option*
:set *option=value*	Assign *value* to *option*
:set no*option*	Deactivate *option*
:set	Display options set by user
:set all	Display list of all current options, both default and those set by the user
:set *option*?	Display value of *option*

* In *.exrc* files, omit colon at the start of *ex* commands.

Other ex Commands (continued)

`:`	Invoke *ex* from *vi* editor
`:vi`	Invoke *vi* editor from *ex*
`:sh`	Invoke shell
`^D`	Return to editor from shell
`:! command`	Give UNIX *command*
`:r newfile`	Read contents of *newfile* into current file
`:r !command`	Read output of UNIX *command* into current file

B

Setting Environment Options

The following table contains brief descriptions of all `set` command options. In the first column, options are listed in alphabetical order; if the option can be abbreviated, that abbreviation is shown in parentheses on the line below. The second column shows the default setting that *vi* uses unless you issue an explicit `set` command (either manually or in the *.exrc* file). The last column describes what the option does, when enabled.

Option	Default	Description
autoindent (ai)	noai	In insert mode, indents each line to the same level as the line above or below. Use with `shiftwidth` option.
autoprint (ap)	ap	Displays changes after each editor command. (For global replacement, displays last replacement.)
autowrite (aw)	noaw	Automatically writes (saves) file if changed before opening another file with `:n` or before giving UNIX command with `:!`.
beautify (bf)	nobf	Ignores all control characters during input (except tab, newline, or formfeed).
directory (dir)	/tmp	Names directory in which *ex* stores buffer files. (Directory must be writable.)
edcompatible	noed-compatible	Uses *ed*-like features on substitute commands.
errorbells (eb)	errorbells	Sounds bell when an error occurs.
exrc (ex)	noexrc	Allows the execution of *.exrc* files that reside outside the user's home directory. (System V only.)
hardtabs (ht)	=8	Defines boundaries for terminal hardware tabs.
ignorecase (ic)	noic	Disregards case during a search.
lisp	nolisp	Inserts indents in appropriate lisp format. ( ), { }, [[, and]] are modified to have meaning for lisp.
list	nolist	Prints tabs as ^I; marks ends of lines with $. (Use `list` to tell if end character is a tab or a space.)

Option	Default	Description
magic	magic	Wildcard characters . (dot), * (asterisk), and [ ] (brackets) have special meaning in patterns.
mesg	mesg	Permits system messages to display on terminal while editing in *vi*.
number (nu)	nonu	Displays line numbers on left of screen during editing session.
open	open	Allows entry to *open* or *visual* mode from *ex*.
optimize (opt)	noopt	Abolishes carriage returns at the end of lines when printing multiple lines, speeds output on dumb terminals when printing lines with leading white space (blanks or tabs).
paragraphs (para)	=IPLPPPQP LIpplpipbp	Defines paragraph delimiters for movement by { or }. The pairs of characters in the value are the names of *nroff/troff* macros that begin paragraphs.
prompt	prompt	Displays the *ex* prompt (:) when *vi*'s Q command is given.
readonly (ro)	noro	Any writes (saves) of a file will fail unless you use ! after the write (works with w, Z Z, or autowrite).
redraw (re)	noredraw	Terminal redraws screen whenever edits are made (in other words, insert mode pushes over existing characters, and deleted lines immediately close up). Default depends on line speed and terminal type. noredraw is useful at slow speeds on a dumb terminal: deleted lines show up as @, and inserted text appears to overwrite existing text until you press ESC.
remap	remap	Allows nested map sequences.

Option	Default	Description
report	=5	Displays a message on the prompt line whenever you make an edit that affects at least a certain number of lines. For example, 6dd reports the message "6 lines deleted."
scroll	=[*1/2 window*]	Amount of screen to scroll.
sections	=SHNHH HU	Defines section delimiters for [[ ]] movement. The pairs of characters in the value are the names of *nroff/troff* macros that begin sections.
shell (sh)	=/bin/sh	Pathname of shell used for shell escape (: !) and shell command (: sh). Default value is derived from shell environment, which varies on different systems.
shiftwidth (sw)	=8	Defines number of spaces in backward (^D) tabs when using the autoindent option.
showmatch (sm)	nosm	In *vi*, when) or } is entered, cursor moves briefly to matching (or {. (If match is not on the screen, rings the error message bell.) Very useful for programming.
showmode	noshowmode	In insert mode, displays a message on the prompt line indicating the type of insert you are making. For example, "Open Mode," or "Append Mode." (System V only.)
slowopen (slow)		Holds off display during insert. Default depends on line speed and terminal type.
tabstop (ts)	=8	Defines number of spaces that a TAB indents during editing session. (Printer still uses system tab of 8.)
taglength (tl)	=0	Defines number of characters that are significant for tags. Default (zero) means that all characters are significant.
tags	=tags */usr/lib/tags*	Defines pathname of files containing tags (see the UNIX tag command.) (By default, system searches */usr/lib/tags* and the file *tags* in the current directory.)

Option	Default	Description
term		Sets terminal type.
terse	noterse	Displays shorter error messages.
timeout (to)	timeout	Keyboard maps "time out" after 1 second.*
ttytype		Sets terminal type.
warn	warn	Displays the warning message, "No write since last change."
window (w)		Shows a certain number of lines of the file on the screen. Default depends on line speed and terminal type.
wrapscan (ws)	ws	Searches wrap around either end of file.
wrapmargin (wm)	=0	Defines right margin. If greater than zero, automatically inserts carriage returns to break lines.
writeany (wa)	nowa	Allows saving to any file.

---

* This option is rarely needed. It's useful only with versions of *vi* that let you map a sequence to several keys (for example, :map zzz 3dw). If you set notimeout, you have unlimited time to type the map command zzz, instead of the one second you normally have.

C

ex commands
Command Syntax
Alphabetical List of Commands

This appendix presents an alphabetical list of *ex* commands, but first, it describes the syntax of *ex* commands.

To enter an *ex* command from *vi*, use this form:

```
: [address] command [options]
```

address is the line number or range of lines that are the object of *command*. If no address is given, the current line is the object of the command.

Address Symbols

In *ex* command syntax, *address* can be specified by any of the following:

1,$	All lines in the file.
x,y	Lines *x* through *y*.
x;y	Lines *x* through *y*, with current line reset to *x*.
0	Top of file.
.	Current line.
n	Absolute line number *n*.
$	Last line.
%	All lines; same as 1,$.
x−n	*n* lines before *x*.
x+n	*n* lines after *x*.
−[*n*]	One or *n* lines previous.
+[*n*]	One or *n* lines ahead.
´*x*	Line marked with *x*.
´ ´	Previous mark.
/*pat*/ or ?*pat*?	Ahead or back to line matching *pat*.

Option Symbols

In *ex* command syntax, *options* might be any of the following:

!	Indicates a variant form of the command, overriding the normal behavior.
count	The number of times the command is to be repeated. *count* cannot precede the command, because a number preceding an *ex* command is treated as a line address. d3 deletes three lines beginning with the current line; 3d deletes line 3.
file	The name of a file that is affected by the command. % stands for current file; # stands for previous file.

Alphabetical List of Commands

In this section, the full name of the *ex* command is listed as the keyword. To the right of each keyword is the syntax, using the shortest abbreviation possible for that command. A brief description follows the syntax.

abbrev   **ab** [*string text*]

Define *string* when typed to be translated into *text*. If *string* and *text* are not specified, list all current abbreviations.

append   [*address*] **a**[!]
                        text

                        .

Append *text* at specified *address*, or at present address if none is specified. Add a ! to switch the `autoindent` setting that will be used during input. That is, if `autoindent` was enabled, ! disables it.

args   **ar**

Print the members of the argument list, with the current argument printed within brackets ([ ]).

change   [*address*] **c**[!]
                        text

                        .

Replace the specified lines with *text*. Add a ! to switch the `autoindent` setting during input of *text*.

copy   [*address*] **co** *destination*

Copy the lines included in *address* to the specified *destination* address. The command t is a synonym for `copy`.

delete   [*address*] **d** [*buffer*]

Delete the lines included in *address*. If *buffer* is specified, save or append the text to the named buffer.

edit   **e**[!] [+*n*] [*filename*]

Begin editing on *filename*. If no *filename* is given, bring in another copy of the current file. Add a ! to edit the new file even if the current file has not been saved since the last change. With the +*n* argument, begin editing on line *n*.

file   **f** [*filename*]

Change the name of the current file to *filename*, which is considered "not edited". If no *filename* is specified, print the current status of the file.

global   [*address*] **g**[!]/*pattern*/[*commands*]

Execute *commands* on all lines which contain *pattern*, or if *address* is specified, all lines within that range. If *commands* are not specified, print all such lines. Add a ! to execute *commands* on all lines *not* containing *pattern*.

insert   [*address*] **i**[!]
text

.

Insert *text* at line before the specified address, or at present address if none is specified. Add a ! to switch the autoindent setting during input of *text*.

join   [*address*] **j** [*count*]

Place the text in the specified range on one line, with white space adjusted to provide two blank characters after a period (.), no blank characters after a), and one blank character otherwise.

k   [*address*] **k** *char*

Mark the given *address* with *char*. Return later to the line with ' x.

list   [*address*] **l** [*count*]

Print the specified lines so that tabs display as ^ I and the
ends of lines display as $.

map   **map** *char commands*

Define a macro named *char* in visual mode with the
specified sequence of commands. *char* is usually a single
character, or the sequence #*n*, representing a function key
on the keyboard.

mark   [*address*] **ma** *char*

Mark the specified line with *char*, a single lowercase
letter. Return later to the line with ' x.

move   [*address*] **m** *destination*

Move the lines specified by *address* to the *destination*
address.

next   **n**[!] [[+*command*] *filelist*]

Edit the next file from the command-line argument list.
Use a r g s to list these files. If *filelist* is provided, replace
the current argument list with *filelist* and begin editing on
the first file; if *command* is given (containing no spaces),
execute *command* after editing the first such file.

number   [*address*] **nu** [*count*]

Print each line specified by *address*, preceded by its buffer
line number. Use # as an alternate abbreviation for
n u m b e r.

open   [*address*] **o** [/*pattern*/]

Enter *open* mode (*vi*) at the lines specified by
address, or at the lines matching *pattern*. Exit open mode
with Q.

preserve   **pre**

Save the current editor buffer as though the system had crashed.

print   [*address*] **p** [*count*]

Print the lines specified by *address*. P is another abbreviation.

put   [*address*] **pu** [*char*]

Restore previously deleted or yanked lines, from named buffer specified by *char*, to the line specified by *address*; if *char* is not specified, the last deleted or yanked text is restored.

quit   **q[!]**

Terminate current editing session. Use ! to discard changes made since the last save. If the editing session includes additional files in the argument list that have not yet been accessed, quit by typing q! or by typing q twice.

read   [*address*] **r** *filename*

Copy the text of *filename* at the specified *address*. If *filename* is not specified, the current filename is used.

read   [*address*] **r** !*command*

Read in the output of *command* into the text after the line specified by *address*.

recover   **rec** [*filename*]

Recover *filename* from system save area.

rewind   **rew[!]**

Rewind argument list and begin editing the first file in the list. Add a ! to rewind even if the current file has not been saved since the last change.

set   se *parameter parameter2* ...

Set a value to an option with each *parameter*, or if no *parameter* is supplied, print all options that have been changed from their defaults. For toggle options, each *parameter* can be phrased as "*option*" or "*nooption*"; other options can be assigned with the syntax, "*option=value*"

shell   sh

Create a new shell. Resume editing when the shell is terminated.

source   so *filename*

Read and execute commands from *filename*.

substitute   [*address*] s [/*pattern*/*repl*/] [*options*]

Replace each instance of *pattern* on the specified lines with *repl*. If *pattern* and *repl* are omitted, repeat last substitution. An option of g substitutes all instances of *pattern* on the line. An option of c prompts for confirmation before each change.

t   [*address*] t *destination*

Copy the lines included in *address* to the specified *destination* address. t is an alias for copy.

tag   [*address*] ta *tag*

Switch the focus of editing to *tag*.

unabbreviate
            una *word*

Remove *word* from the list of abbreviations.

undo   u

Reverse the changes made by the last editing command.

unmap   **unm** *char*

Remove *char* from the list of macros.

v   [*address*] **v**/*pattern*/[*commands*]

Execute *commands* on all lines *not* containing
pattern. If *commands* are not specified, print all such
lines. **v** is equivalent to **g**!.

version   **ve**

Print the current version number of the editor and the date
the editor was last changed.

visual   [*address*] **vi** [*type*] [*count*]

Enter visual mode at the line specified by *address*. Exit
with **Q**. *type* can be one of −, ^, or . (See the **z** command). *count* specifies an initial window size.

visual   **vi** [+*n*] *filename*

Begin editing on *filename* in visual mode.

write   [*address*] **w**[!] [[>>] *filename*]

Write lines specified by *address* to *filename*, or full contents of buffer if *address* is not specified. If *filename* is
also omitted, save the contents of the
buffer to the current filename. If >> *filename* is used,
write contents to the end of the specified *filename*. Add a
! to force the editor to write over any current contents of
filename.

write   [*address*] **w** !*command*

Write lines specified by *address* to *command*.

wq   **wq**[!]

Write and quit the file in one movement.

xit   **x**

Write file if changes have been made to the buffer since last write, then quit. x is equivalent to **wq**.

yank *[address]* **ya** *[char] [count]*

Place lines specified by *address* in named buffer indicated by *char*, or if no *char* is specified place in general buffer.

z   *[address]* **z** *[type] [count]*

Print a window of text with line specified by *address* at the top. *type* can be one of:

+ Place specified line at the top of the window (default).

− Place specified line at bottom of the window.

. Place specified line in the center of the window.

^ Print the window before the window associated with type −.

= Place specified line in the center of the window and leave the current line at this line.

count specifies the number of lines to be displayed.

!   *[address]* **!***command*

Execute *command* in a shell. If *address* is specified, apply the lines contained in *address* as standard input to *command*, and replace the lines with the output.

=   *[address]* **=**

Print the line number of the line indicated by *address*.

< >   [*address*] < [*count*]

             or

             [*address*] > [*count*]

             Shift lines specified by *address* in specified direction.
             Only blanks and tabs are shifted in a left-shift (<).

address   *address*

             Print the lines specified in *address*.

RETURN   RETURN

             Print the next line in the file.

&   [*address*] & [*options*] [*count*]

             Repeat the previous substitute command.

~   [*address*] ˜ [*count*]

             Replace the previous regular expression with the previous
             replacement pattern from a substitute command.

D

Problem Checklist

Problems Opening Files
Problems Saving Files
Problems Getting to Visual Mode
Problems with vi Commands
Problems with Deletions

This appendix consolidates the problem checklists that are provided throughout the text. Here they are presented in one place for ease of reference.

Problems Opening Files

√ *When you invoke* vi, *the message* [open mode] *appears.*

Your terminal type is probably incorrectly identified. Quit the editing session immediately by typing :q and ask your system administrator to provide an adequate terminal type setting.

√ *You see one of the following messages:*

```
Visual needs addressable cursor or upline capability
Bad termcap entry
Termcap entry too long
terminal:  Unknown terminal type
Block device required
Not a typewriter
```

Your terminal type is either undefined, or there's probably something wrong with your *termcap* or *terminfo* entry. Enter : q to quit. Then ask your system administrator to select a terminal type for your environment.

√ *A* [new file] *message appears when you think a file already exists.*

You are probably in the wrong directory. Enter : q to quit. Then check to see that you are in the correct directory for that file (enter pwd at the UNIX prompt). If you are in the right directory, check the list of files in the directory (with ls) to see whether the file exists under a slightly different name.

√ *You invoke* vi, *but you get a colon prompt (indicating that you're in* ex *line-editing mode).*

You probably typed an interrupt before *vi* could draw the screen. Enter *vi* by typing vi at the *ex* prompt (:).

√ *One of the following messages appears:*

```
[Read only]
File is read only
Permission denied
```

"Read only" means that you can only look at the file; you cannot save any changes you make. You may have invoked *vi* in *view mode* (with view or vi -R), or you do not have write permission for the file. See the section "Problems Saving Files" below.

√   *One of the following messages appears:*

```
Bad file number
Block special file
Character special file
Directory
Executable
Non-ascii file
file non-ASCII
```

The file you've called up to edit is not a regular text file.

√   *When you type* :q *because of one of the above difficulties, the message appears:*

```
No write since last change (:quit! overrides).
```

You have modified the file without realizing it. Type :q! to leave *vi*. Your changes from this session will not be saved in the file.

Problems Saving Files

√   *You try to write your file, but you get one of the following messages:*

```
File exists
File file exists - use w!
[Existing file]
File is read only
```

Type :w! *file* to overwrite the existing file, or type :w! *newfile* to save the edited version in a new file.

√   *You want to write a file, but you don't have write permission for it. You get the message "Permission denied."*

Use :w! *newfile* to write out the buffer into a new file. If you have write permission for the directory, you can use *mv* to replace the original version with your copy of it. If you don't have write permission for the directory, type :w! *pathname/file* to write out the buffer to a directory in which you do have write permission (such as your home directory).

√ *You try to write your file, but you get a message telling you that the file system is full.*

Type : ! d£ to see whether there's any space on another file system. If there is, choose a directory on that file system and write your file to it with : w ! *pathname*. (Starting an *ex* command with an exclamation point gives you access to UNIX, and d£ is the UNIX command to check a *disk's free* space.)

√ *The system puts you into open mode and tells you that the file system is full.*

The disk with *vi*'s temporary files is filled up. Type : ! ls /tmp to see whether there are any files you can remove to gain some disk space. If there are, create a temporary UNIX shell from which you can remove files or issue other UNIX commands. You can create a shell by typing : sh; type [CTRL-D] or exit to terminate the shell and return to *vi*. (On a Berkeley UNIX system, you can simply type [CTRL-Z] to suspend *vi* and return to the UNIX prompt; type % to return to *vi*.) Once you've freed up some space, write your file with : w ! .

√ *You try to write your file, but you get a message telling you that your disk quota has been reached.*

Try to force the system to save your buffer with the *ex* command : pre (short for : preserve). If that doesn't work, look for some files to remove. Use : sh (or [CTRL-Z] if you are using a Berkeley system) to move out of *vi* and remove files. Use [CTRL-D] (or %) to return to *vi* when you're done. Then write your file with : w ! .

Problems Getting to Visual Mode

√ *While editing in vi, you accidentally end up in the ex editor.*

A Q in the command mode of *vi* invokes *ex*. Any time you are in *ex*, the command : vi returns you to the *vi* editor.

Problems with vi Commands

√ *When you type commands, text jumps around on the screen and nothing works the way it's supposed to.*

You may have hit the CAPS LOCK key without noticing it. *vi* is case-sensitive. That is, uppercase commands (I, A, J, etc.) are different from lowercase commands (i, a, j), so all your commands are being interpreted not as lowercase but as uppercase commands. Press the CAPS LOCK key again to return to lowercase, then type either U to restore the last line changed or u to undo the last command. You'll probably also have to do some additional editing to fully restore the garbled part of your file.

Problems with Deletions

√ *You've deleted the wrong text and you want to get it back.*

There are several ways to recover deleted text. If you've just deleted something and you realize you want it back, simply type u to undo the last command (for example, a dd). This works only if you haven't given any further commands, since u only undoes the most recent command.

You can still recover a recent deletion, however, by using the p command, since *vi* saves the last nine deletions in nine numbered deletion buffers. If you know, for example, that the third deletion back is the one you want to restore, type:

    "3p

to "put" the contents of buffer number 3 on the line below the cursor.

This works only for a deleted *line*. Words, or a portion of a line, are not saved in a buffer. If you want to restore a deleted word or line fragment, and u won't work, use the p command by itself. This restores whatever you've last deleted.

Index

A

abbreviation command, 112-113
  avoiding loops, 113
  disabling, 113
  for multiple lines, 115
  listing current definitions, 113
addresses, of lines, 62
append, after cursor (a), 19
  to end of line (A), 33
  to existing files (:w >>), 70
autowrap, 12, 14, 32, 107

B

buffers, numbered, 54
  preserve (:pre), 54
  recovering after a crash, 53-54
  recovering numbered, 27, 55
  renaming files, 69
  saving commands in, 123
  yanking to named, 54-56

C

CAPS LOCK key, 35
change, character (r), 22-23
line (cc), 22, 33
text (c), 2, 20, 35, 50
text from cursor to end of line
(C), 22
word (cw), 20-21
characters, deleting (see vi commands)
command mode, 2, 11
commands, vi (see vi commands)
copy, range of lines (:co or :t), 63
text (y); see also yank, 2, 16,
29-30, 35, 50
text (yank and put), 29-30
crash, recovering from, 53-54
cursor movement, by character
(h, j, k, l), 13, 35
by line (+, -), 41
by line number (G), 46-47
by repeating searches (n, N), 44
by screen, 38
by search for a pattern (?, /),
42-43
by text block, 41
by word (w, b), 35
by word (w, b), 15-16
search within current line (f, t),
45-46
to marked place in file, 57
using numeric arguments, 14
within a line (0, $), 14-15, 35
within a screen (H, M, L), 40

D

delete, all blank lines, 90
character (x), 26
line (dd), 25
range of lines (:d), 63
text (d), 23, 30, 35, 50
to end of line (D), 26
to end of sentence, 42
word (dw), 24-25
deletions, recovering, 54;
from numbered buffers, 27, 55;
with undo, 27
diff command (UNIX), 131-134
display, current line number (^G),
46-47
line numbers (:set nu), 15, 47
line(s) (ex editor), 60
dumb terminal, 18, 25

E

editing, combining movement, 21,
50
commands (see vi commands; ex
commands)
editor, line, 1, 59;
screen, 1
(see also vi editor; ex editor)
entering vi, (see opening a file or
vi commands)
ESCAPE key, 11
/etc/termcap file, 103
ex commands, 58-75, 139-145,
151-160
abbreviate words (:ab), 112-113
allow metacharacters (:set
magic), 107
allow other .exrc files (:set exrc),
106

append to existing files (:w >>), 70

call in next of multiple files (:n), 73

combining with vertical bar, 68, 116

confirm substitutions, 78

context-sensitive replacement, 77, 79-80

copy lines (:co), 62

define paragraphs (:set para=), 42

define sections (:set sect=), 42

define shiftwidth (:set sw=), 136

define tabs (:set ts=), 135

define window size (:set w=), 104

delete lines (:d), 62

display line numbers (:set nu), 15, 47

display line (:p), 60

display tabs (:set list), 136

edit multiple files (:e), 72-73

execute UNIX commands from vi, 108-112

filter text through UNIX command, 109-112

for loop with, 126-128

global (:g), 76

global search (:g), 67

here documents, 128

ignore case (:set ic), 85

indent input (:set ai), 135

invoke on a file, 59

invoke vi (:vi), 60

line addressing symbols, 64

map command sequence, 114-123

map function keys, 121-122

match brackets (:set sm), 137

move lines (:m), 62

move text blocks by patterns, 87

number lines (:set nu), 63

pattern matching, 80-101, 89-101

preserve a buffer (:pre), 54

quit file (:q), 68

quit without saving edits (:q!), 6-7, 68

read in a file (:r), 70-71

replace in text block, 87

save, 112

save and exit files, 68

save in buffer, 123

save part of a file, 69

save under new filename, 69

scripts, 124-134;
     built by diff, 131-134

search for class of words, 87

search patterns, 65

set ignorecase (:set ic), 104, 107

set vi options, 103-107, 104

set wrapmargin (:set wm=), 12, 14, 32

set wrapscan (:set ws), 45

sort text blocks, 129-130

substitute (:s), 60, 76

syntax of, 3

use from within vi, 60

wrap searches (:set ws), 107

wrap words (:set wm=), 107

write (save) and quit file (:wq), 68

write (save) and quit file (:x), 68

write (save) file (:w), 68

yank text between files, 74

ex editor, introduction to, 1, 3, 58
     (see also ex commands)

EXINIT variable, 103

.exrc file, 103, 105

F

files, append to existing, 70
call in next of multiple, 73
editing between, 74
editing multiple, 71-72
invoking vi on multiple, 71
marking a place in, 57
opening, 3-6
quit, 68
quit and save edits, 6, 8, 35, 68
quit without saving edits, 6-7, 35, 68
reading in, 70-71
save as new, 69
saving, 6, 68
saving part of, 69
(see also vi commands)
filter text through a UNIX command, 109-112
for loop, 126-128
function keys, mapping, 121-122

G

general form of vi commands, 21
global replacement, 76-101
collecting lines, 99-101
confirming, 78
context-sensitive, 77, 79-80
delete blank lines, 90
delete variable text string, 95-96
different character as pattern delimiter, 89
inserting lines, 115
lines that don't match, 93
on text blocks, 87
one or more characters, 90, 94
pattern matching, 80-101, 89-101

repeat an ex command, 99
reverse line order, 93
reverse word order, 92, 96-99
search for class of words, 87
simple, 77, 79
undoing, 78
uppercase conversion, 89, 92, 95
whole word, 85-86, 89

H

here documents, 128

I

indent, automatic in insert mode, 135-136
insert, at beginning of line (I), 33
on new line (O, o), 33
text (i), 2, 11, 18
insert mode, 11
mapping, 120
intelligent terminal, 18

J

joining lines (J), 34

L

line addresses, 62
absolute, 63
redefining current line, 66
relative, 64
search patterns, 65
symbols, 64

line editor, 1, 59
  (see also ex editor)
loop, repetition of ex script,
  126-128

M

mapping, commands, 114-123
  examples, 116-121;
    editing multiple files, 118;
    repeating long insertion, 119;
    reusing a valid command key,
      117;
    surrounding word with font
      codes, 118;
    transposing words, 117
  function keys, 121-122
  insert mode, 120-122
  keys unused in vi, 114
  quoting special characters, 115
  special keys, 123
mark a place in a file (m), 57
metacharacters, in replacement
  strings, 83-85
  in search patterns, 81-83
mode, command, 2, 11
  insert, 11, 120
  read-only, 52
move, combining with edit command, 21, 50
  range of lines (:m), 63
  text (delete and put), 27-28, 30

N

numeric arguments, with edit
  commands, 21
  with insert commands, 34
  with movement commands, 14

O

opening a file, 3-6

P

pattern matching, (see search;
  global replacement)
problem checklist, 161-165
put text (P, p), 27, 29-30, 35,
  55-56

Q

quick reference, vi and ex,
  139-145
quit, file (:q), 68
  saving edits; :wq, 68;
  :x, 68;
  ZZ, 6, 8, 35
  without saving edits (:q!), 6-7,
  35, 68

R

reading in files, 70-71
read-only mode, 52
recovering, buffers after a system
  crash, 53-54

deletions, 54;
from numbered buffers, 27, 55;
with u, 27
redrawing the screen, 39
regular expressions, in replacement strings, 83-85
in search patterns, 81-83
renaming buffers, 69
repeating last vi command (.), 31
replace, character (r), 22-23
overstriking characters (R), 33
text (see global replacement)

S

saving files, 6
(see also vi commands)
screen editors, 1
(see also vi editor)
scripts, 124-134
built by diff, 131-134
comments in, 130
sort text blocks, 129-130
(see also ex commands)
scrolling, 38
with cursor stationary (z), 39
search, and replace, 79
and replace within text block, 87
backward for a pattern (?), 44
combine opening a file with, 51
for general class of words, 87
global (see global replacement)
ignoring case, 85, 104, 107
matched brackets, 136-137
metacharacters treated like normal characters, 107
pattern (/), 42-43
pattern matching, 80-101
repeat (n, N), 44, 78

within current line, 45-46
wrapping around file, 45, 107
set options, allow metacharacters
in searches (:set magic), 107
alphabetical list of, 146-150
assign a value, 104
autoindent (:set ai), 135
display tabs (:set list), 136
exrc, 106
ignore case (:set ic), 104, 107
inquire about options, 104-105
number lines (:set nu), 15, 47, 63
paragraphs (:set para=), 42
sections (:set sect=), 42
shiftwidth (:set sw=), 136
show matching brackets (:set
sm), 137
tabstop (:set ts=), 135
turn on or off, 104
window size (:set w=), 104
wrapmargin (:set wm=), 12, 14,
32, 107;
map example, 119
wrapscan (:set ws), 45, 107
shell, commands, execute from vi,
108-112
script; for loop, 126-128;
here documents, 128
sort, text blocks, 129-130
substitute, character (s), 33
line (S), 33
text (:s), 33, 60
system crash, recovering from,
53-54

T

tags, for C code, 137-138
terminal, dumb, 18, 25

intelligent, 18
operations; /etc/termcap/file,
103;
termcap, 122;
terminfo, 122
text blocks, sorting, 129-130
switching, 87
text editor, (see editor)
text object, 21, 35
filter through command, 109
transposing, characters (xp), 29
words, 117

U

undoing, all vi commands on a
line (U), 32
last vi command (u), 27, 31-32,
78
UNIX commands, compare files
(diff), 131-134
execute from vi, 108-112
filter text through, 109-112

V

vi, entering (see opening a file, or
vi commands)
invoking on multiple files, 71
vi commands, abbreviated words,
112-113
append text (a), 16, 19
append text to end of line (A), 33
case sensitivity of, 3
change character (r), 22-23
change lines (cc), 22, 33
change text (c), 2, 16, 20, 35, 50
change text to end of line (C), 22

change words (cw), 20-21
combine edits and movement, 50
command mode, 11
copy text, 16
copy text (yank and put), 29-30,
55
copy (yank and put) text, 56
copy (yank) text (y), 2, 16,
29-30, 35, 50
delete character (x), 26
delete line (dd), 25
delete text (d), 16, 23, 30, 35, 50
delete to end of line (D), 26
delete word (dw), 24-25
display current line number (^G),
46-47
filter text through UNIX command, 109-112
@-functions, 123
general form, 21
insert mode, 11
insert text at beginning of line (I),
33
insert text (i), 2, 11, 16, 18
join lines (J), 34
mapped to function keys,
121-122
mapping, 114-123
mark a place in file (m), 57
move cursor by character, 13, 35
move cursor by line, 41
move cursor by screen, 38
move cursor by text block, 41
move cursor by word, 15-16, 35
move cursor to line number n
(nG), 46-47
move cursor within a line, 14-15,
35
move cursor within a screen, 40
move text, 16

move text (delete and put), 27-30
numeric arguments with; edit
   commands, 21;
   insert commands, 34;
   movement commands, 14
open file, 3-6;
   at a specific place, 51;
   in read-only mode, 52
open line for text (O, o), 33
put text before cursor (P), 27, 30,
   55-56
put text (p), 16, 27, 29-30, 35,
   55-56
quick reference to, 139-145
quit and save edits (ZZ), 6, 8, 35
recover buffers after system
   crash, 53-54
recover deletions with u, 27
recover numbered buffers (deletions), 27, 55
repeat last command (.), 31, 78
repeat search (n, N), 44, 78
replace character (r), 22-23
replace characters (R), 33
save, 112
save in buffer, 123
scroll screen with cursor stationary (z), 39
search backward for pattern (?),
   44
search for pattern (/), 42-43
search within current line, 45-46
stop inserting text (ESC), 11
substitute character (s), 33
substitute line (S), 33
summary of, 35
transpose characters (xp), 29
undo all edits to line (U), 32
undo last edit (u), 27, 31-32, 78
yank; text between files, 74-75;

text (y), 16, 29-30, 35, 50
   to named buffers, 54-56
vi editor, alternate environments,
   103, 105
customizing, 103-107;
   (see also set options)
execute UNIX commands from,
   108-112
introduction to, 1-9

W

wildcard characters, (see metacharacters)
window size, 104
word abbreviation, 112-113

Y

yank, text (y), 2, 29-30, 35, 50
   text between files, 74
   to named buffers, 54-56

Colophon

Our look is the result of reader comments, our own experimentation, and distribution channels.

Distinctive covers complement our distinctive approach to UNIX documentation, breathing personality and life into potentially dry subjects. UNIX and its attendant programs can be unruly beasts. Nutshell Handbooks help you tame them.

The animal featured on the cover of *Learning the vi Editor* is a tarsier.

Edie Freedman designed this cover and the entire UNIX bestiary that appears on other Nutshell Handbooks. The beasts themselves are adapted from 19th-century engravings from the Dover Pictorial Archive.

Linda Lamb designed the page layout for the Nutshell Handbooks. The text of this book is set in Times Roman; headings are Helvetica®; examples are Courier. Text was prepared using SoftQuad's *sqtroff* text formatter. Figures are produced with a Macintosh™. Printing is done on an Apple LaserWriter®.